BORROWED TIME

BORROWED TIME

Photographs by Caroline Vaughan

FOREWORD BY REYNOLDS PRICE

For Cathy
Hoping she will remember
Caroline Vaughan 9/21/97

DUKE UNIVERSITY PRESS Durham and London 1996

Typeset in ITC Carter and Cone Galliard
Printed in the USA by Litho Inc on acid free paper
Library of Congress Cataloging-in-Publication Data
appear on the last printed page of this book.

This book is dedicated to Steve and Ruth Wainwright.

FOREWORD
GROUNDS TO STAND ON

by Reynolds Price

It may well be no coincidence that the invention of photography occurred in the midst of the flood tide of the European novel—the best work of Dickens, Charlotte and Emily Brontë, Tolstoy, Dostoevsky, Balzac, and Flaubert (to name only a few) overlaps the birth and early youth of the single image imprinted by daylight alone on a sensitized surface. For while photography is most often considered an outgrowth of centuries of sculptural and graphic mimesis—more or less realistic statues, drawings, and paintings—it seems equally possible that the immense power of visual imagery implicit in the indelible characters and scenes of the great nineteenth-century novels worked as an instigator on the pioneers of photography.

Perhaps that immense well of successfully imitative language, and the realer-than-real worlds of so many distinguished prose narrators, served to ignite a few amateur scientist/artists toward the creation of a parallel and equally potent medium (it's beyond doubt, for instance, that nineteenth-century fiction and drama played crucial roles in the development of the motion picture; and a film artist of the depth of Sergei Eisenstein demonstrated in a memorable essay the cinematic prophecies of Milton's *Paradise Lost*).

Who, reading *Anna Karenina* or *Madame Bovary*, doesn't soon long for an actual likeness of each of those beautiful doomed women and clear reflections of the rooms and skies under which each sought her escape from a fate she was simultaneously and furiously weaving for herself? Despite the virtual disappearance, in the past fifty years, of illustrations from serious works of fiction, who wouldn't be interested in seeing, say, Gustav Nadar's illustrations for *Bovary*, Cecil Beaton's for *Anna*; or to come further onward, Walker Evans's for John Updike's Rabbit novels and Eudora Welty's for Toni Morrison's *Beloved*, not to speak of Henri Cartier Bresson's for almost anything in any language?

In fact, if I were given the choice of a single artist to illustrate a deluxe edition of, say, my own novel, *Kate Vaiden*, I would choose Caroline Vaughan. Not because she was a gifted member of a freshman class in narrative writing which I taught at Duke in 1968 nor because our friendship has continued to grow through ensuing decades as we've lived and worked together in the same town. I'd choose her for *Kate* because she shares, to an uncanny degree, my character's piercingly dry and unblinking vision and because, from her earliest apprentice work, Caroline Vaughan has managed the rare feat of incorporating our unquenchable human impulse to narrate—to tell stories—within her most potent single images. Even more remarkably, she has mastered the linking together of long runs of discrete images on the all but invisible chain of an uninsistent but headlong narrative.

Any thoughtful watcher would gain from at least a few minutes' exercise in studying the entire surface of a Vaughan image and coaxing a story out of its givens of illumination, place, summoned atmosphere, and living creatures (if any). Pictures on the order of "Constructivist Double Portrait," "An LaBarre, Bonnie and Jody," or even a near-abstract yet familiar sight like "Magnolia" would be fruitful subjects for almost anyone's careful witness—a careful patient witness in the hope, first, of building a story of one's own from the given facts and then, perhaps, of slowly guessing the arc of the narrative voice which is unavoidably implicit in the artist's own scrutiny of a person or thing whose time she has briefly borrowed.

Borrowed Time. What kinds of *time?* And *borrowed* in what sense? Most obviously, the *time* consists of those minutes or hours during which a living creature or an inanimate object is detained, studied, and registered on film. The simplest *borrowing* consists of the time demanded from a sitter's actual lifespan and in the photographer's demand for the living subject's emotional cooperation and for the live tree's or dead rock's stasis (after his release from prison, Oscar Wilde enjoyed taking pictures with a simple camera, and in a late letter he summarizes the finding of most of his fellow photographers when confronted with allegedly fixed subjects—"I'm concentrating on cows. Cows love to be photographed; and what's more—unlike architecture—they never move").

The simplest return which Vaughan can offer to the sitter for his time borrowed is the finished image itself, preserved not merely in a memorably arrested moment but enhanced by the darkroom skills of a printer without superior among contemporary artists. She has even pointed out, by way of an aside, how often the time devoted to her photography must be borrowed from the responsibilities of acquiring funds to continue her work (she has never lived on the proceeds of her pictures).

But given Vaughan's determination, her technical virtuosity, and the painlessly invasive depth of her scrutiny, it seems entirely possible that her best pictures of the living have borrowed all of a given sitter's past (every day of his or her history) plus a sizable piece of a particular creature's central vitality or soul and that she endows him in return with an altered but faithful image, floated on paper, which seems likely to prove watchable for at least a relative eternity.

I call them faithful images because, while I have known a number of her sitters and have sat for her often myself, I've never known Vaughan to attempt either visual flattery or the scarifying detraction that invalidates the work of so many others. She's a devourer, to be sure, but a benign devourer, transformer, and epitomizer of the actual world. And anyone who believes the camera incapable of falsehood should see how a few of her subjects fare in the photographs of others. Out of Vaughan's reach, each face invariably seems less alive, less likely to thrive beyond the frozen moment.

But here, though we have more than sixty self-sufficient images, we have also a selection from the prolific work of more than two decades. Her drastic selection, from many hundreds of possibilities, is offered to the watcher as a progression—an ongoing rhythm whose goal is simultaneously intellectual, emotional, and narrative. For by intermixing pictures from nearly twenty-five years of work, Vaughan has required the watcher to respond either to her own story, as it's silently imbedded in an image, or to a story of his or her own invention.

Any stories that I may have deduced from individual pictures, or from the entire arrangement, will unavoidably say more about me than the images or their inherent subjects; so I'll stay well out of the watcher's path. I will, though, note what a watcher may not surmise from Vaughan's laconic captions—that she has begun and ended with her eagle-eyed father, that images of her benignly wary mother and of her parents together provide other turning points in the sequence, that many of the most recent pictures study both orthodox and unorthodox human couples, and that mute nature (the world of flowers, rocks, streams) is a hummingly live and intimate player and witness throughout.

In the number of Vaughan's pictures which are devoid of human beings, the inanimate or animate-but-mute things portrayed are watching the photographer and the photographer's later surrogate—you and me—with an intensity so strict that they'd threaten to pronounce a judgment on our lives and minds if Vaughan's choices of stance, distance, and the tone of her light did not imbue all her subjects with her own grave tolerance of the world's masks and faces (her pictures seldom accept the randomly offered light of a given day; they wait for their proper time).

To be sure, a detailed narrative was no conscious part of Vaughan's intent when the pictures were arranged in their present order. It's my own suggestion that a great many possible stories lie before a close watcher, and that the building of a story—a refinement of the second most important human pleasure—can sharpen and deepen a watcher's experience of the collection. Vaughan's own conscious principle of organization was largely emotional. The initial picture of her father by the huge bare tree—a picture whose blurred crescent top suggests the subject's own vision, as cataracts cloud the lenses of his own eyes—is the first hint of a quiet refrain of *memento mori* which hovers throughout. *The world is this various, this beautiful, this appalling; it will soon expel or enfold us all.*

Even more so than a portrait, a landscape painting, or a sound recording, every photograph—both here and elsewhere—is its own flayed skull. However calming or eye-stopping its subject, a photograph is unavoidably its own assertion of the mortality of all creation: sometimes the mortality of people and things already lost to us, sometimes of the achingly young and vulnerable (the fact that a photograph of the dying composer Frédéric Chopin survives from 1849 is at least as eerily surprising as the invention of one more postponer of death by drug researchers). For modern lenses and emulsions have steadily reduced the length of the moment in which an image is caught and held; and the instant in which that image is borrowed from life becomes a unique survivor.

The instant itself becomes an archeological prize quite different from all the other forms of preservation and survival available, from cave paintings to Cinerama to the wonders of Egyptian mummification and American undertaking. And since most of Vaughan's pictures imply elaborate prior calculations of pose, light, and angle, her results are as unlike snapshots—or skilled news photographs—as her medium permits.

Yet the intensity of the emotional content of each Vaughan image dispels any suggestion of frigid or overcooked perfection. Only an artist helplessly fascinated by her subject, if not in outright love with the person or thing pursued, could return from the world with pictures so technically masterful and yet so resonant of a care as steady and formidable as any hawk's of its nested young. Among her pictured couples, for instance, I know that one couple consists of two brothers, one of whom hoped to be changed into a woman and is now dead. One member of another couple is dying of AIDS; another consists of an older man and a younger who have nonetheless lived together for more than twenty loyal years.

Yet Vaughan's captions withhold such knowledge from the watcher, as I withhold specific identifications here—it is part and parcel of the artist's concern that you meet these honored faces directly, with no prior baggage of approval or rejection. If you deduce certain forms of strangeness from appearances, if some of them repel or disturbingly attract you, then you've made your own fresh story from visual evidence—*What's the story you've told about yourself? Is it as remotely humane as the story Vaughan has offered?* If you see the two brothers, for instance, as a husband and wife, then that understandable story becomes both an index to your sensibility and a question about your keenness, your tolerance. What has art ever been for but to lure all watchers, then test them down to the bone and marrow?

Against a good deal of twentieth-century fashion, Vaughan has always hunted down beauty in the world. Her lilies and pomegranates, nude women, Christ-like men and streams—though more blessedly opulent than most of us expect to meet in nature—are easy enough to sweep unthinkingly into that memory-bag we each call "Beautiful Sights." It's harder work, watching some of her couples, waiting in their presence till a whole distinct being flowers and states its name and purpose on the common Earth. Corpulent, maimed, self-victimized, or simply monumentally homely—how do they differ from a million pictures in dime-store frames on American shelves: Uncle Dave and Aunt Elma, Jim and Tim, Eve and Sandra?

First, to be sure, they differ in the brand of skill with which they're recorded.

Second, they appear not at their own request but on the photographer's invitation. For reasons of her own, Vaughan has wanted to honor their faces and bodies, to borrow that moment which stands a chance of being the actual bud of their fullness, the instant that's ready to part its doors and show a patient watcher the strongest claim a solitary human or a human pair can make on our own time, our fellow feeling, our humblest mercy. Her pictures of individual faces are even more urgently charged with their demand, a demand made silently and slowly in a picture that—think of the strangeness of the complex transaction—we readily know as a fellow member of a sizable species, presently dominant on the planet, though not guaranteed for an infinite run.

So for more than two decades—while holding down a daily job that has no apparent relation with her work, through trials as earnest as most of us bear if we outlast the cradle—Caroline Vaughan has firmly persisted in a hungry aim that rose in her early. Her first papers in my course in freshman composition at Duke were intensely imagistic; but before she was much further on in her life, words had proven inadequate for her particular need. She was quickly off and passing through the hands of mentors as useful as Imogen Cunningham and Minor White as she searched the world—the palpable world in most of its guises—with visual tools, plus ample infusions of her sleepless curiosity. Her luck in possessing an inborn admiration and thanks for our common world—her fear of and trust in our visible round of things and people—required both exploration and capture in sights of her own making: a few of which sights are laid down for us here, an alternate world yet worthy of trust.

It's a realm I've trusted through trials of my own. When I feel myself rusting, corroding, flagging in a gray stretch of chores and repeated failure—worn by the blunt knocks of time on my own balky skull—the sight of any one of a number of photographs by Caroline Vaughan can clean my sight like a fierce but soon forbearing solvent. In her work, the Earth is its full best self—a self from all its billion selves, all things to all creatures: terror and joy, our hope of rescue, our eventual rest.

BORROWED TIME

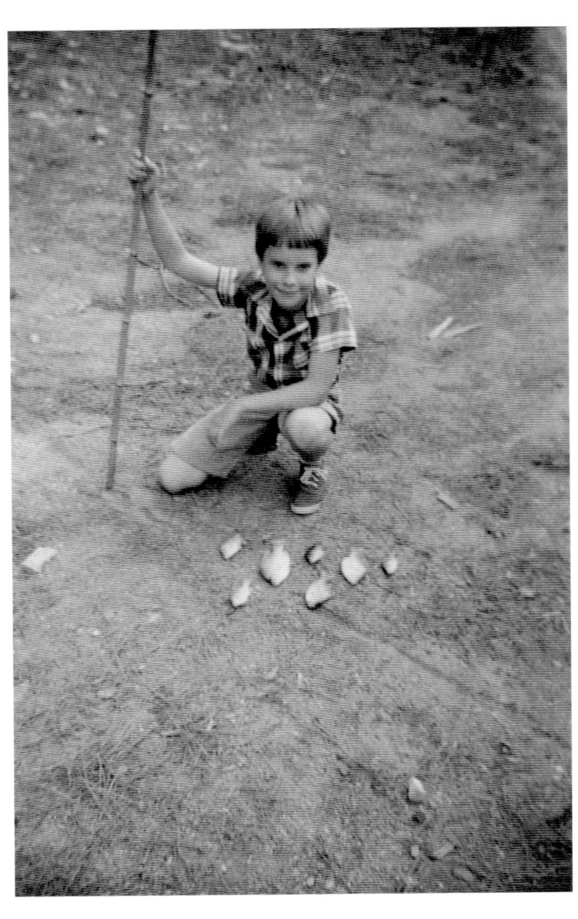

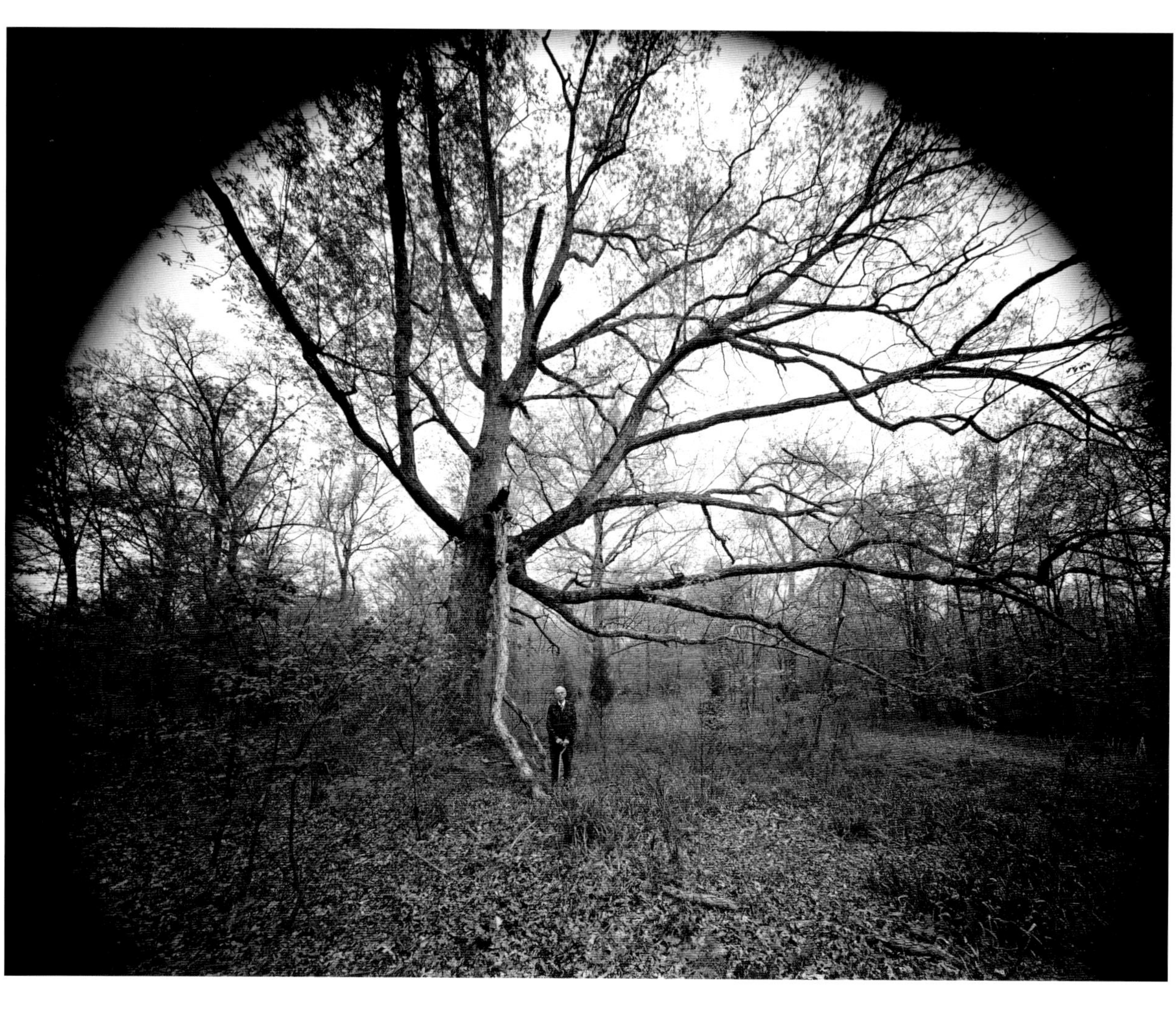

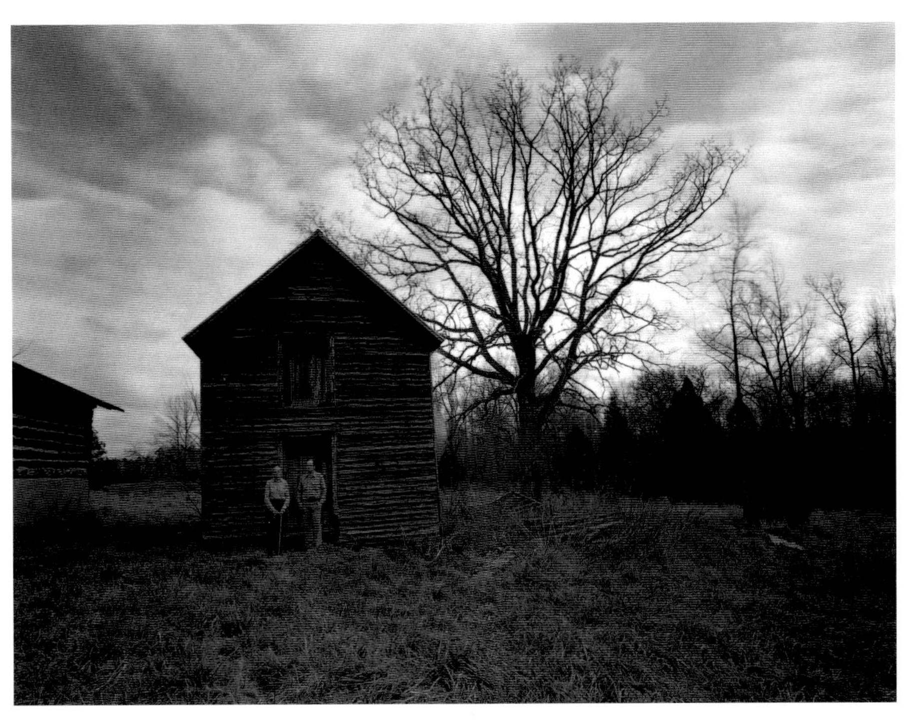

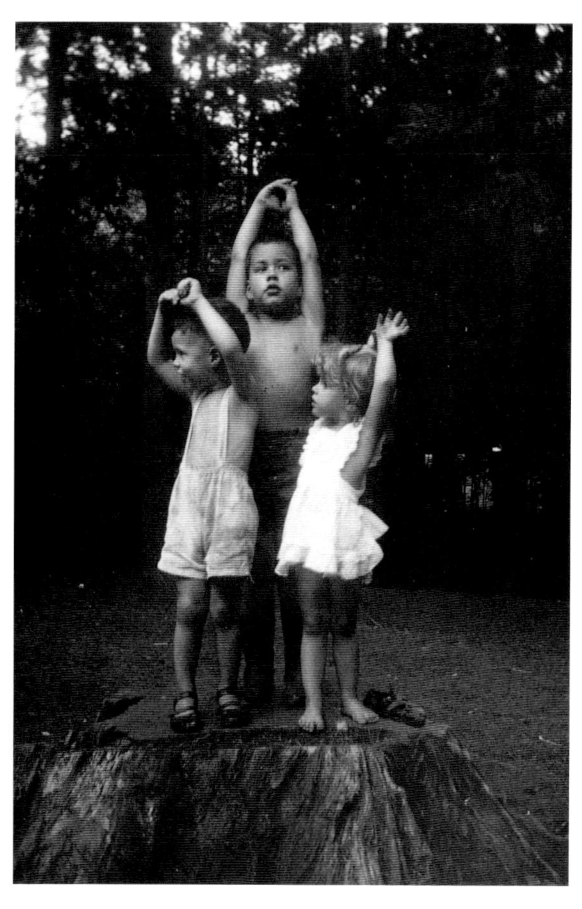

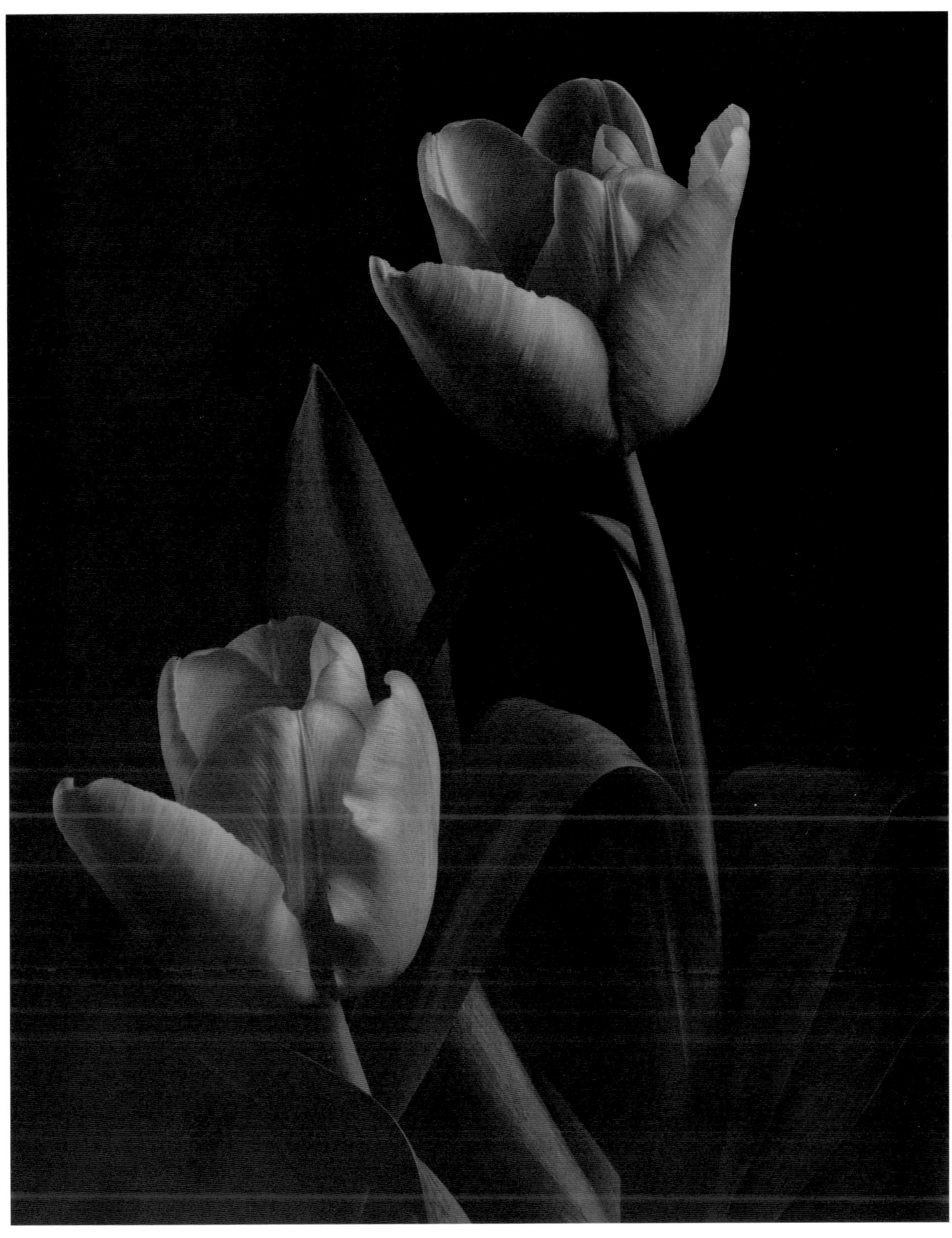

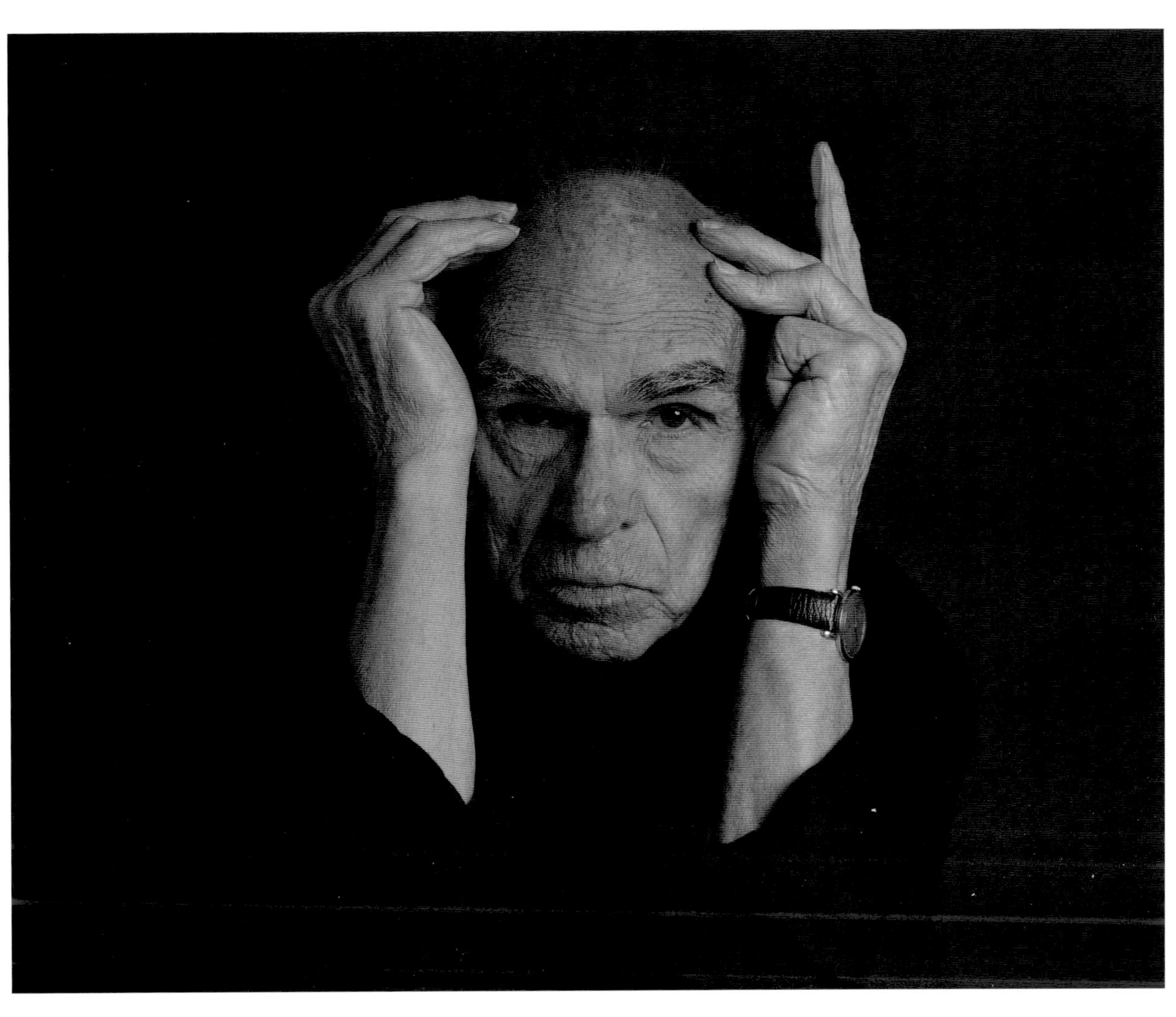

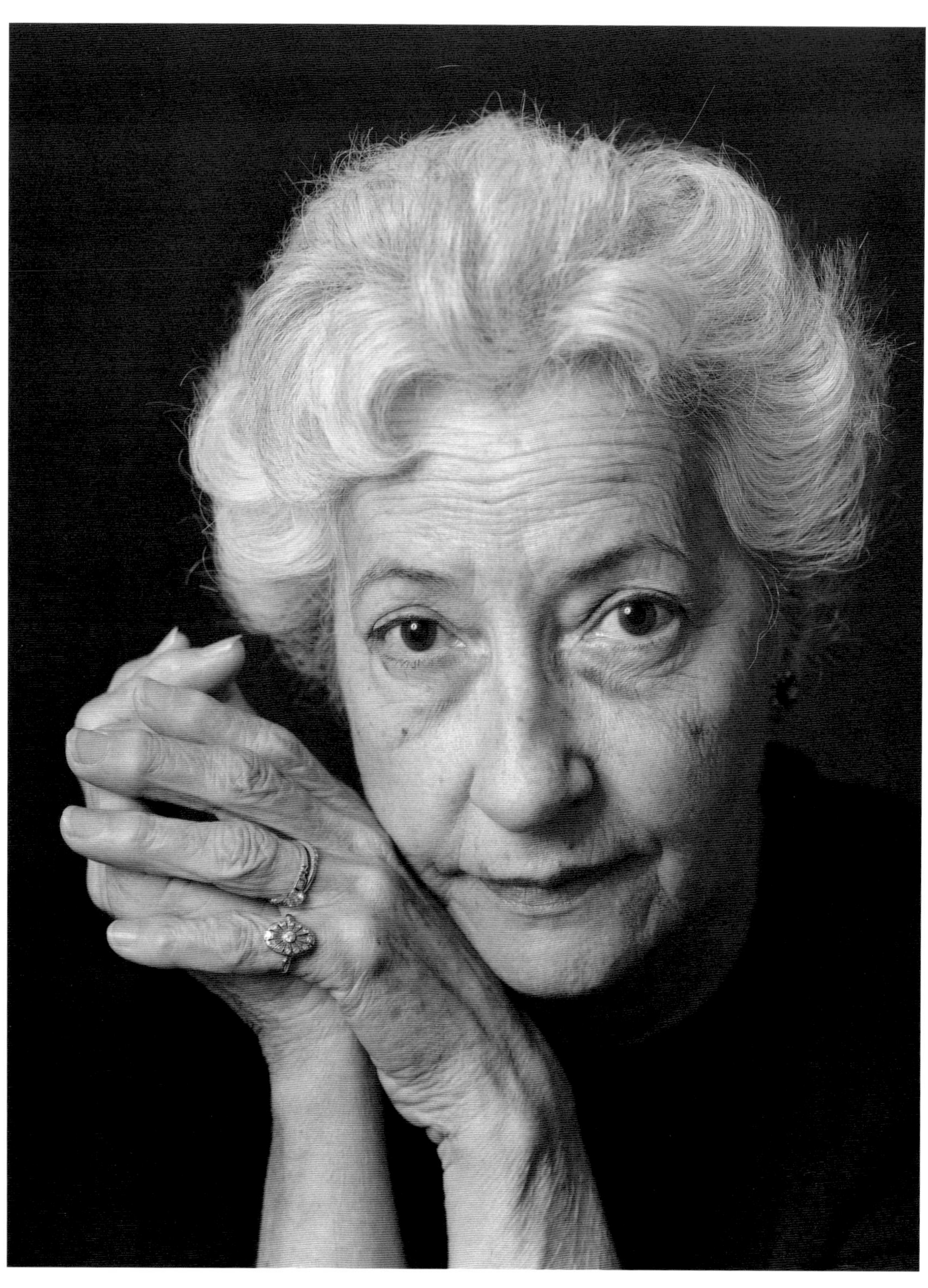

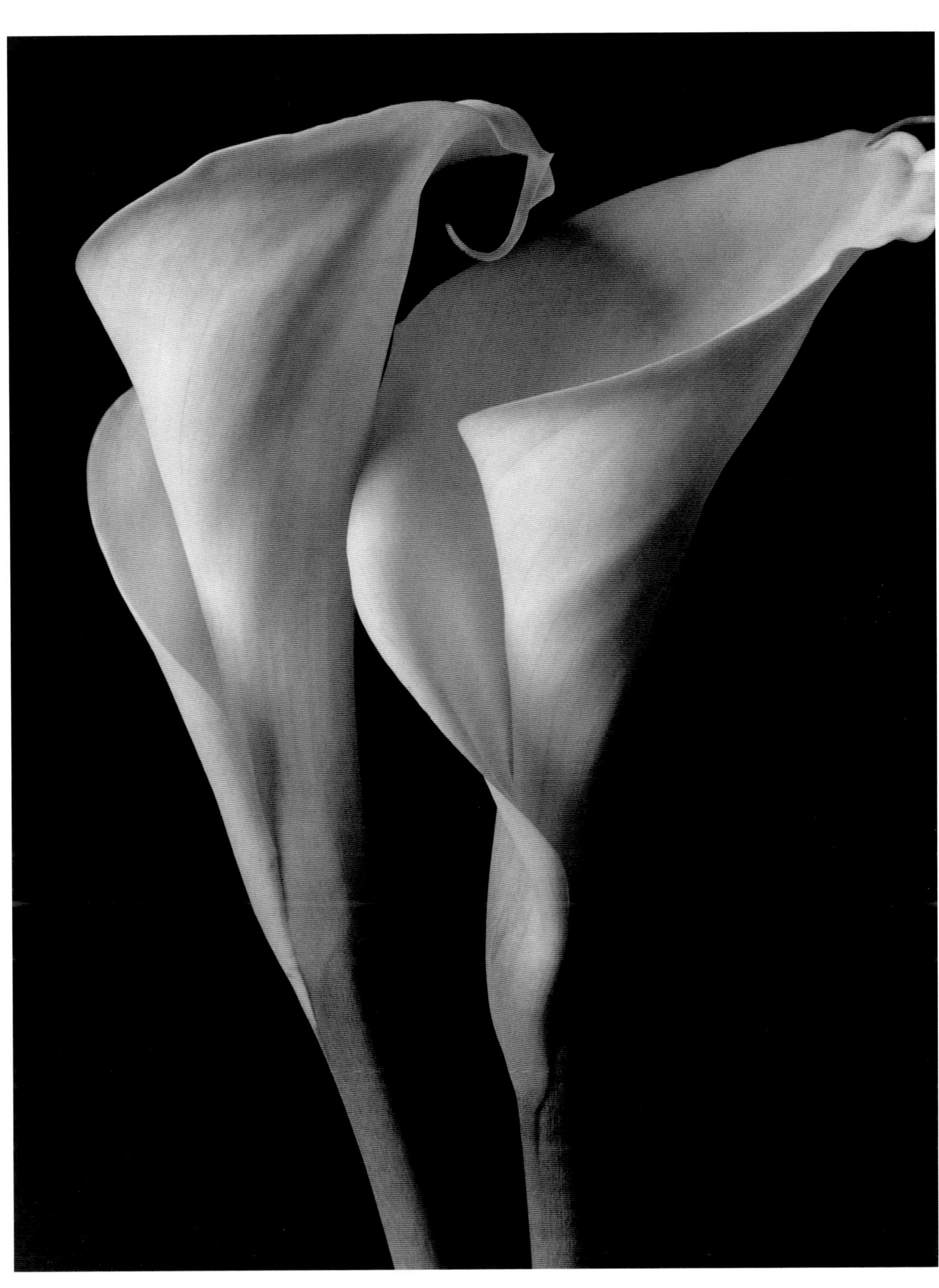

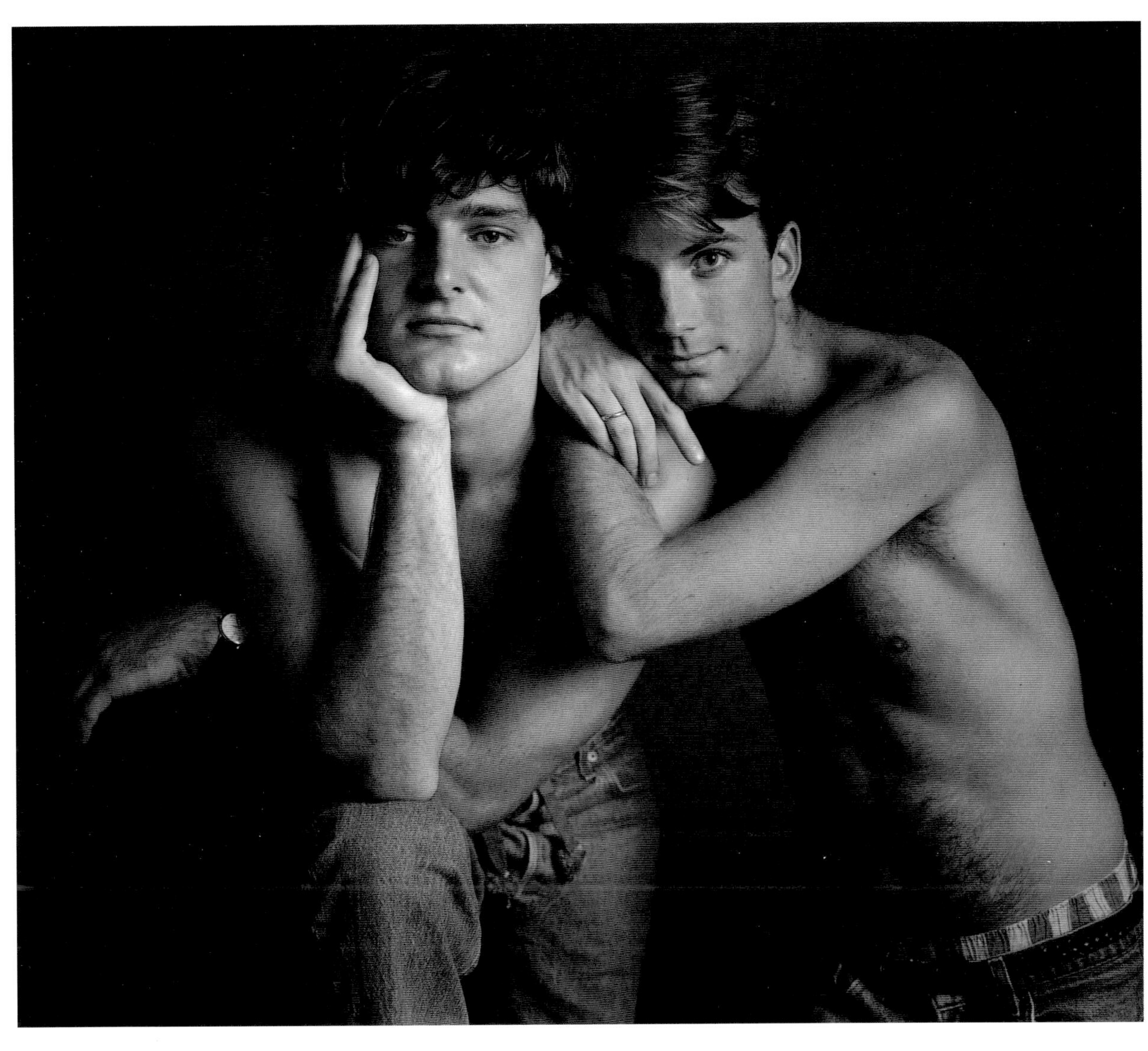

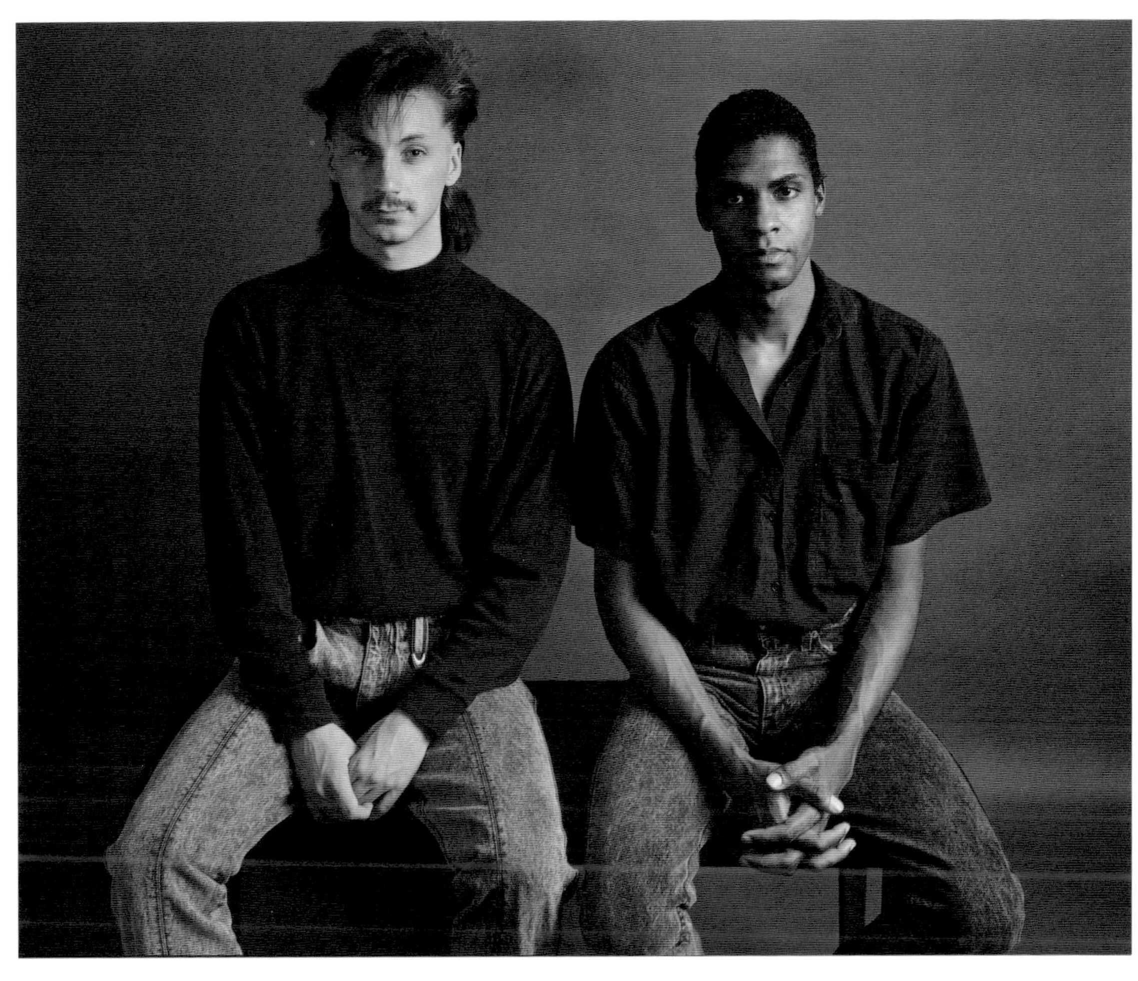

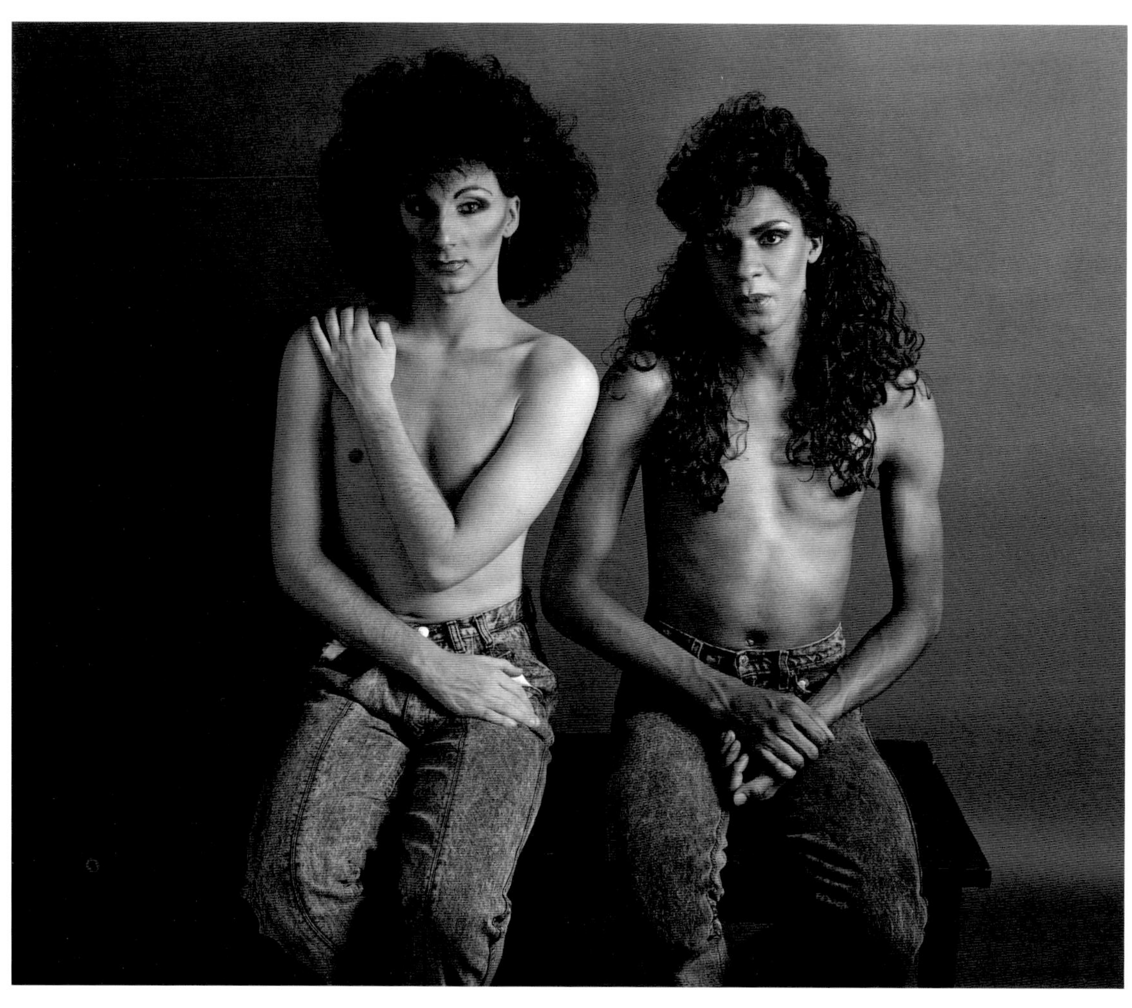

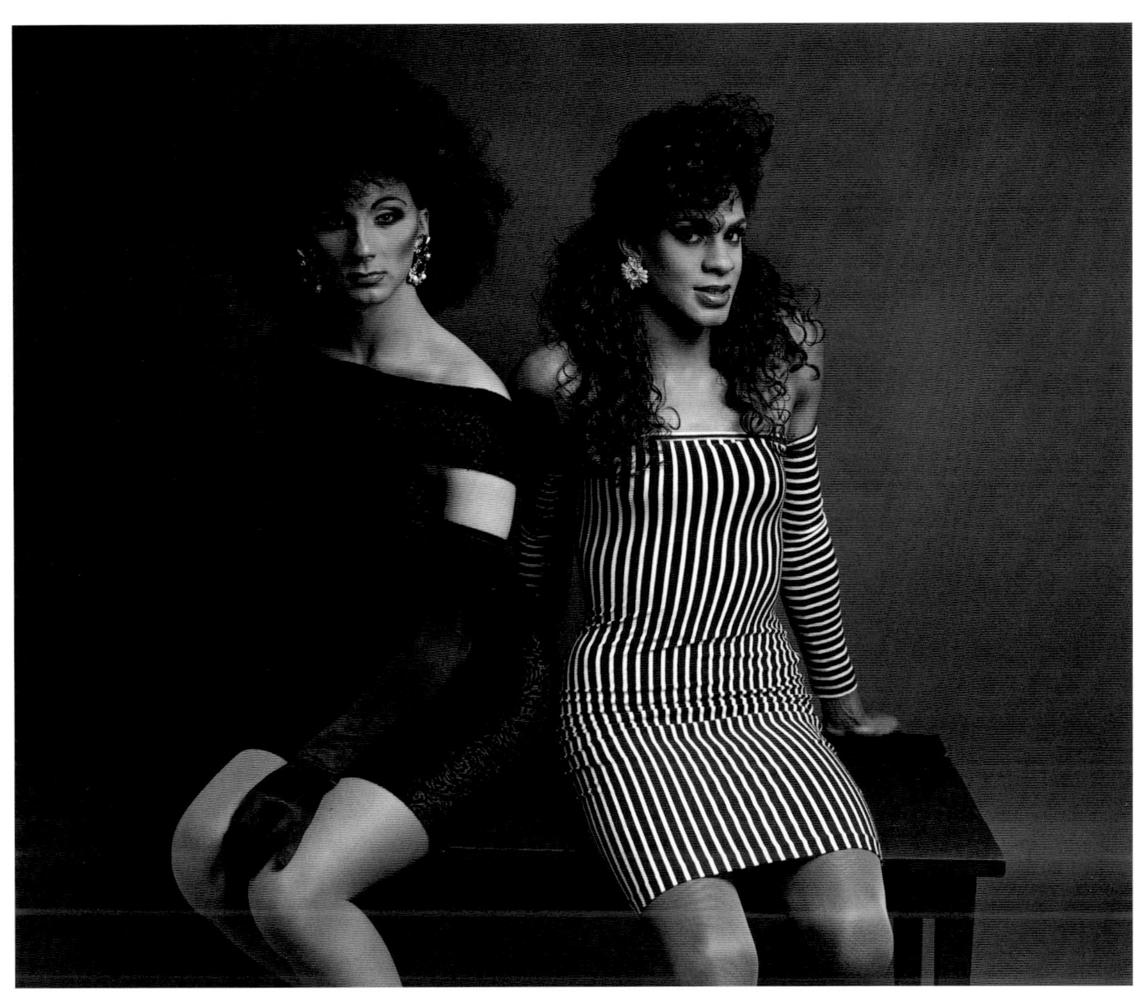

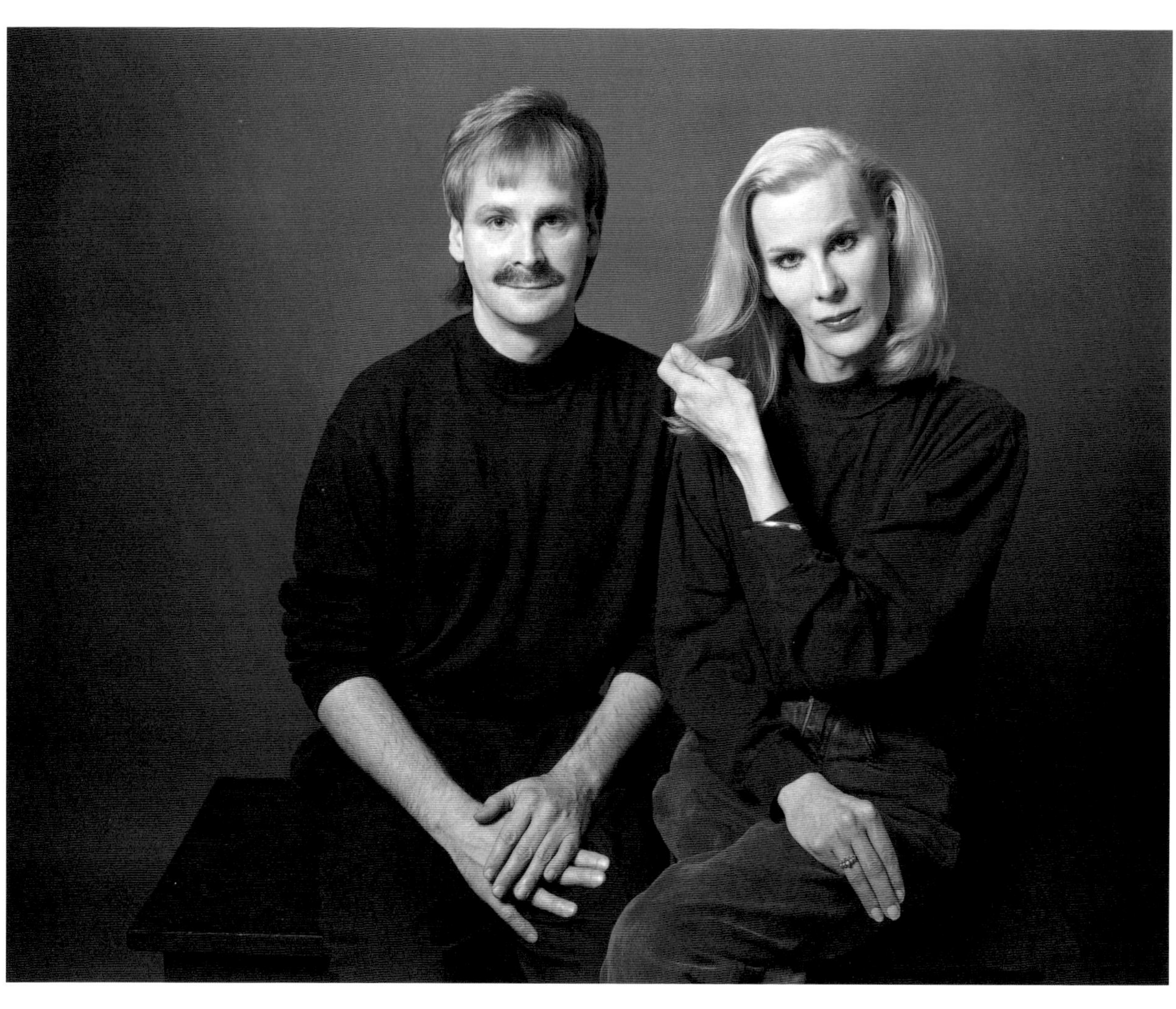

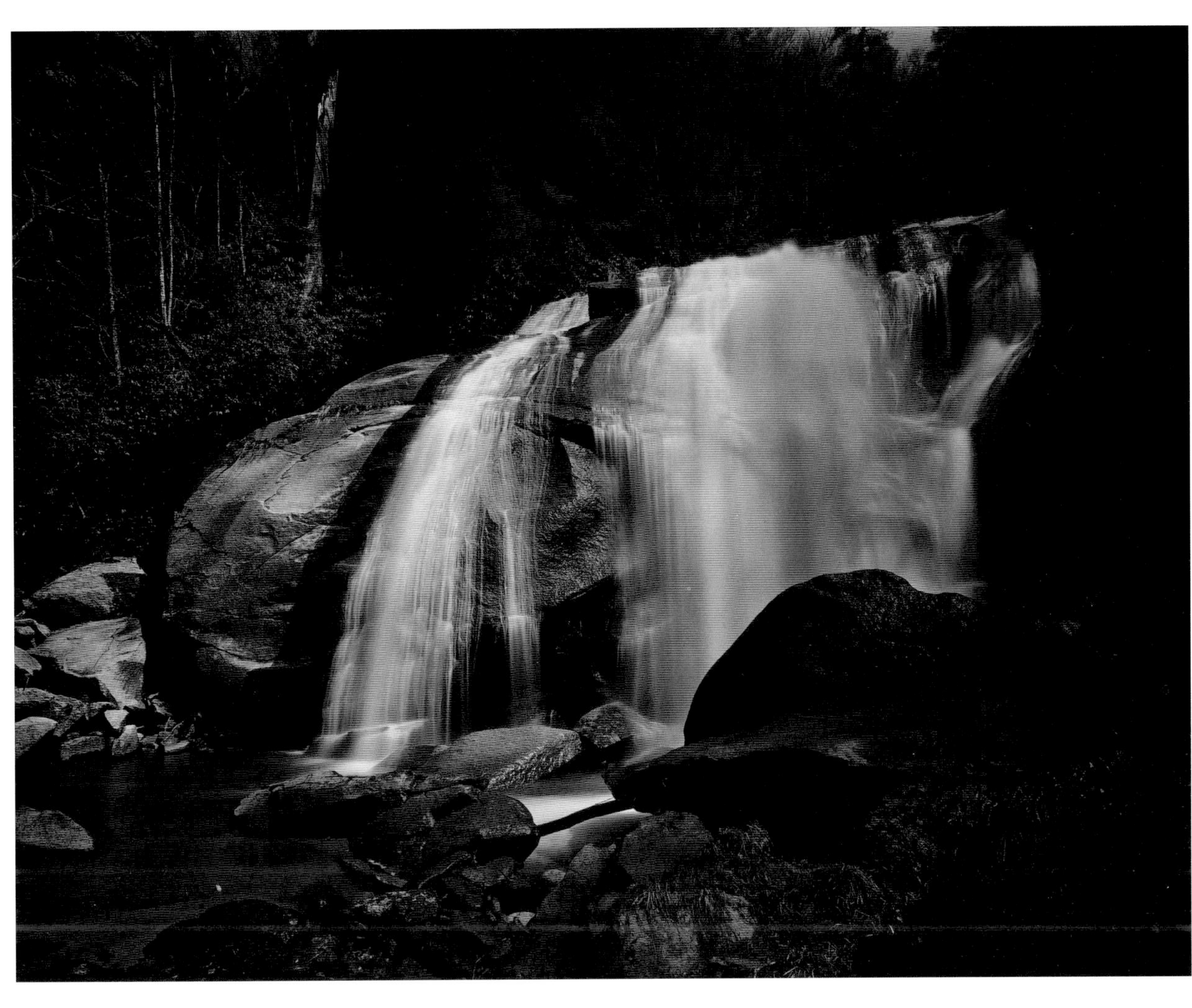

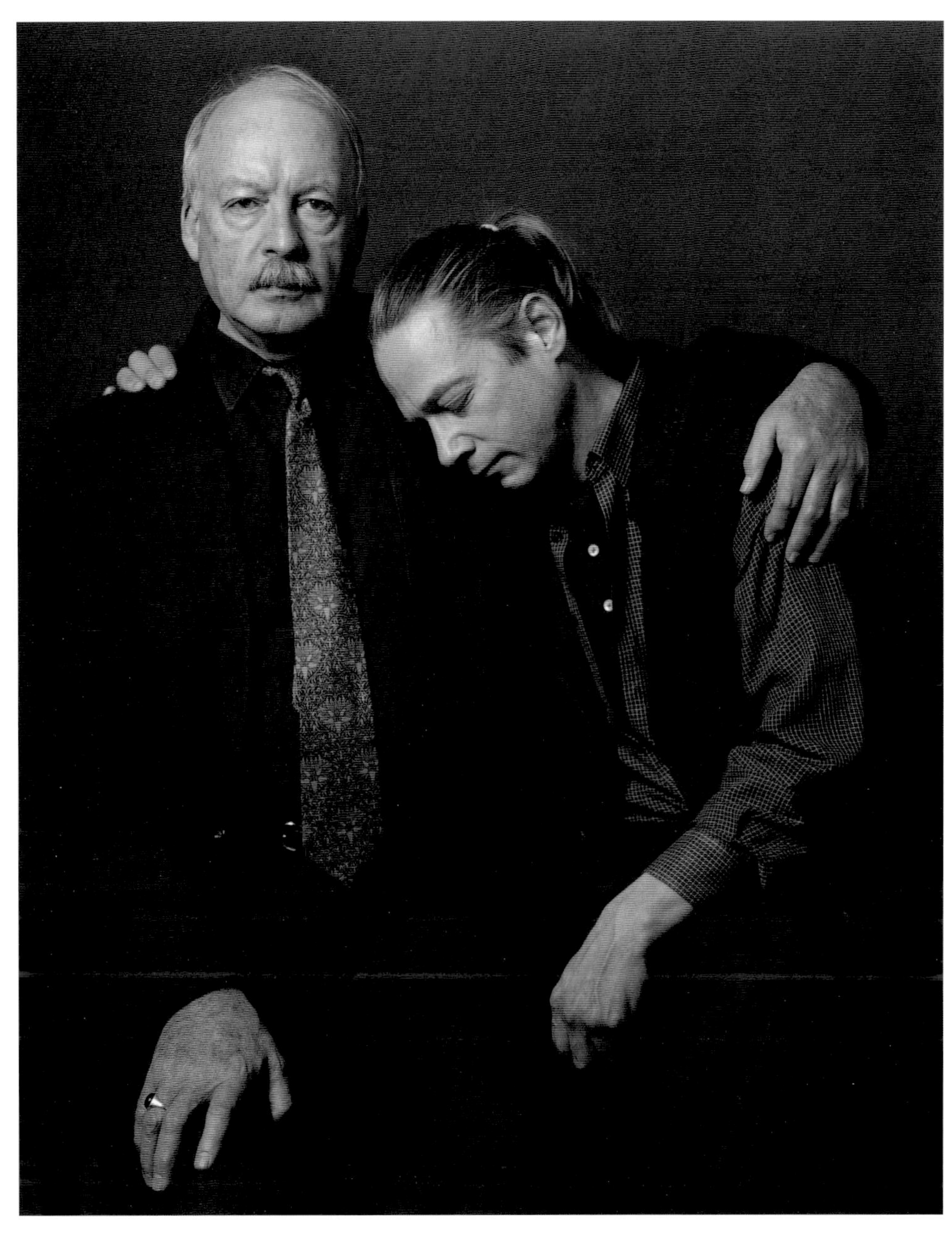

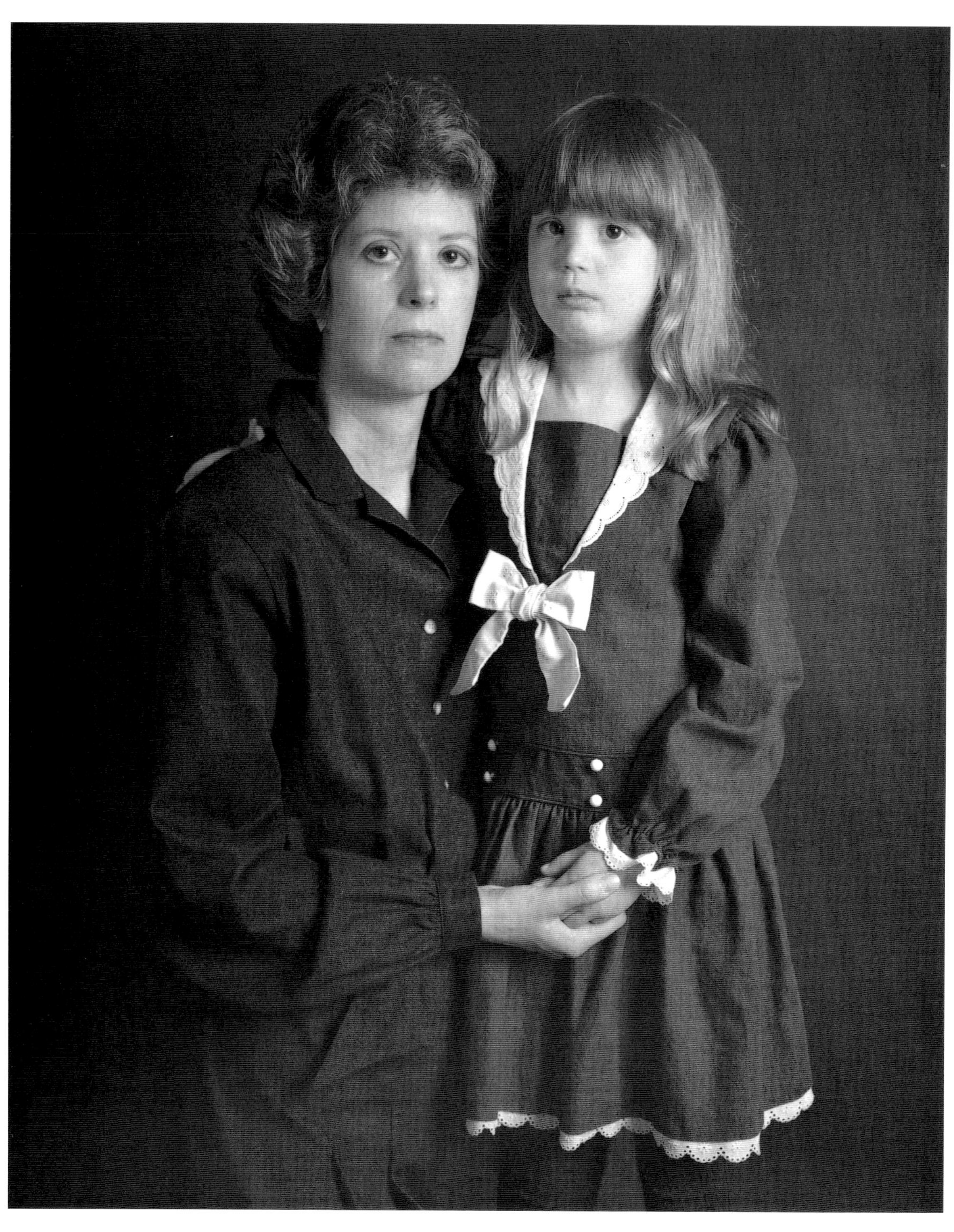

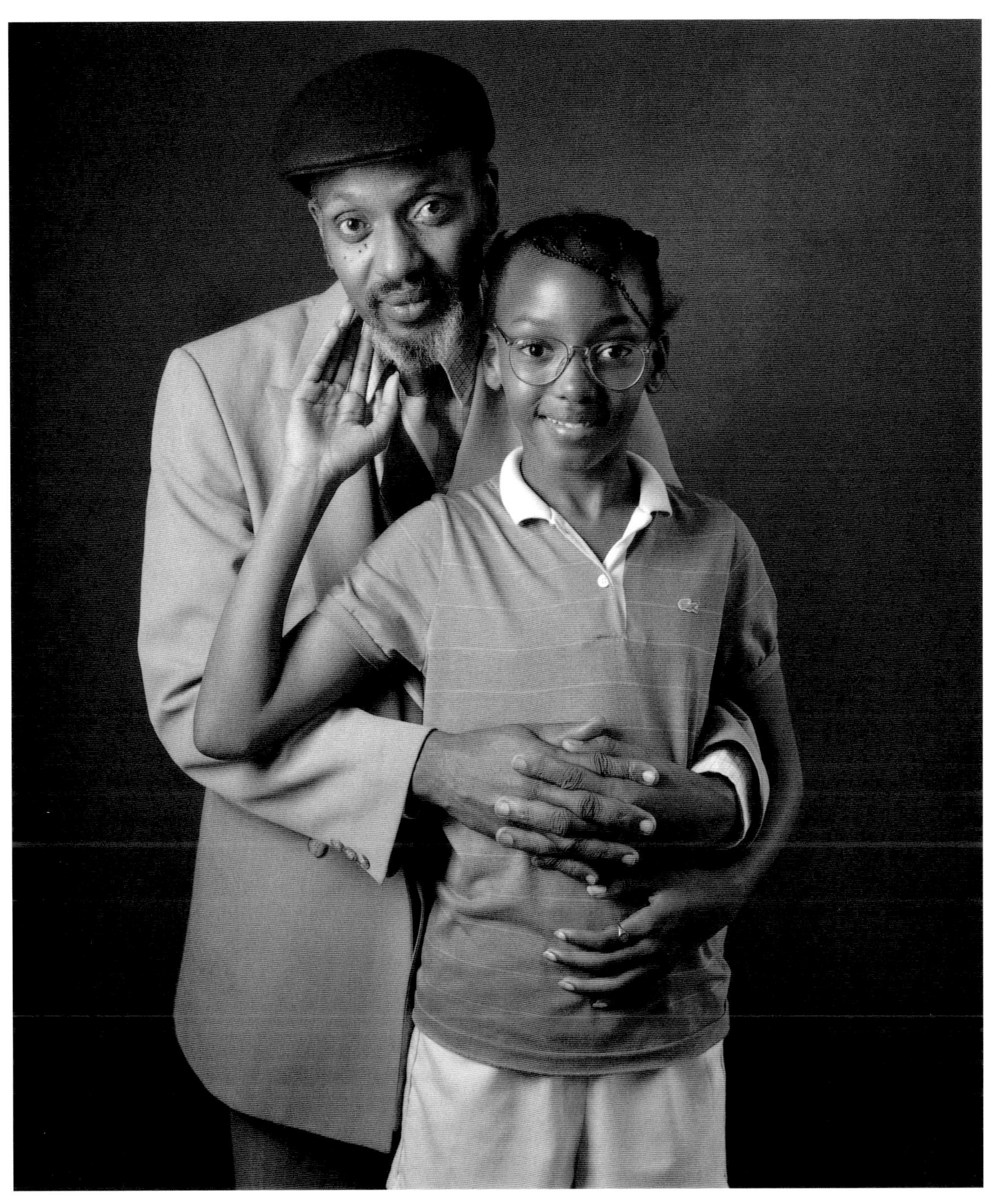

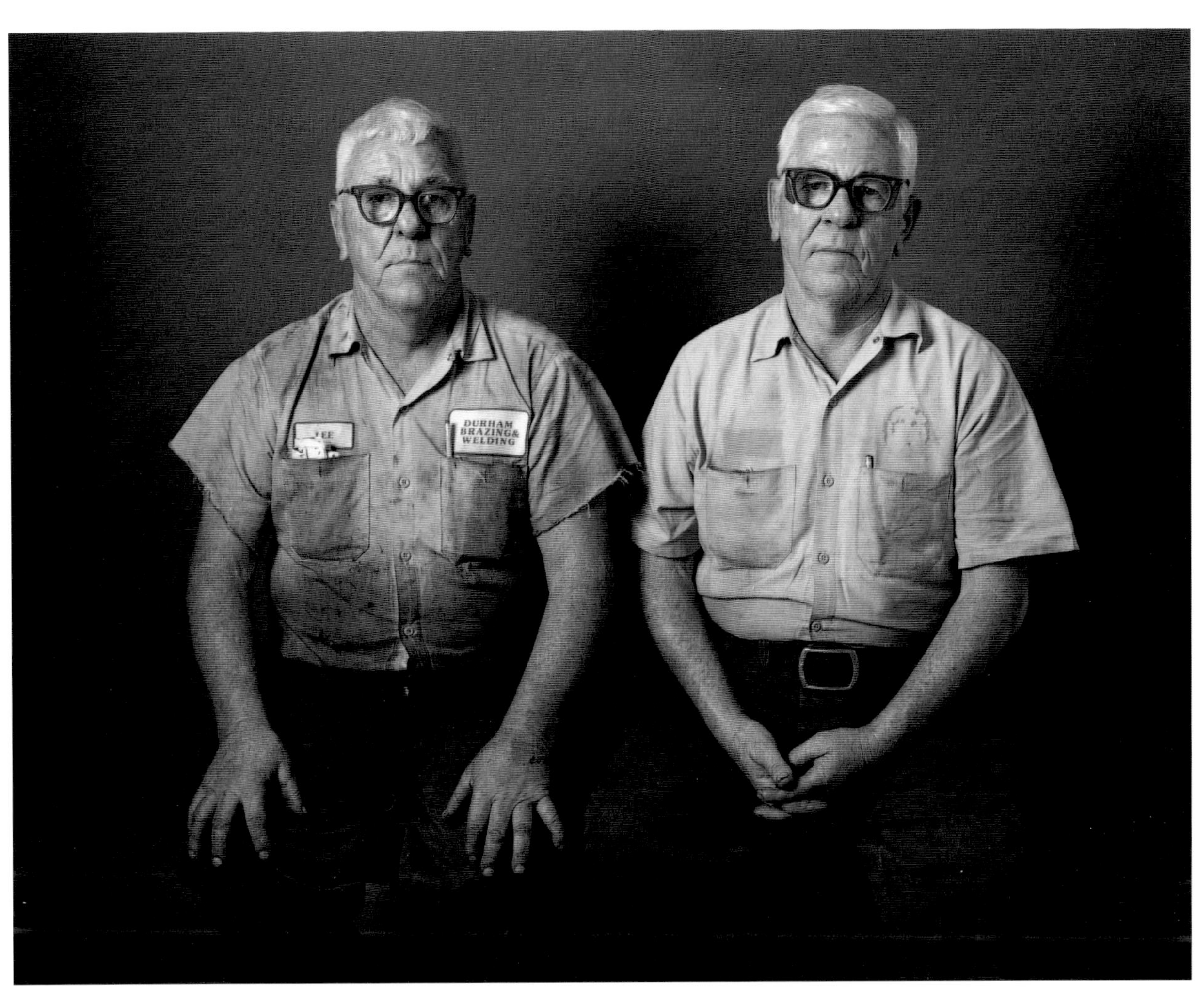
DURHAM
BRAZING&
WELDING

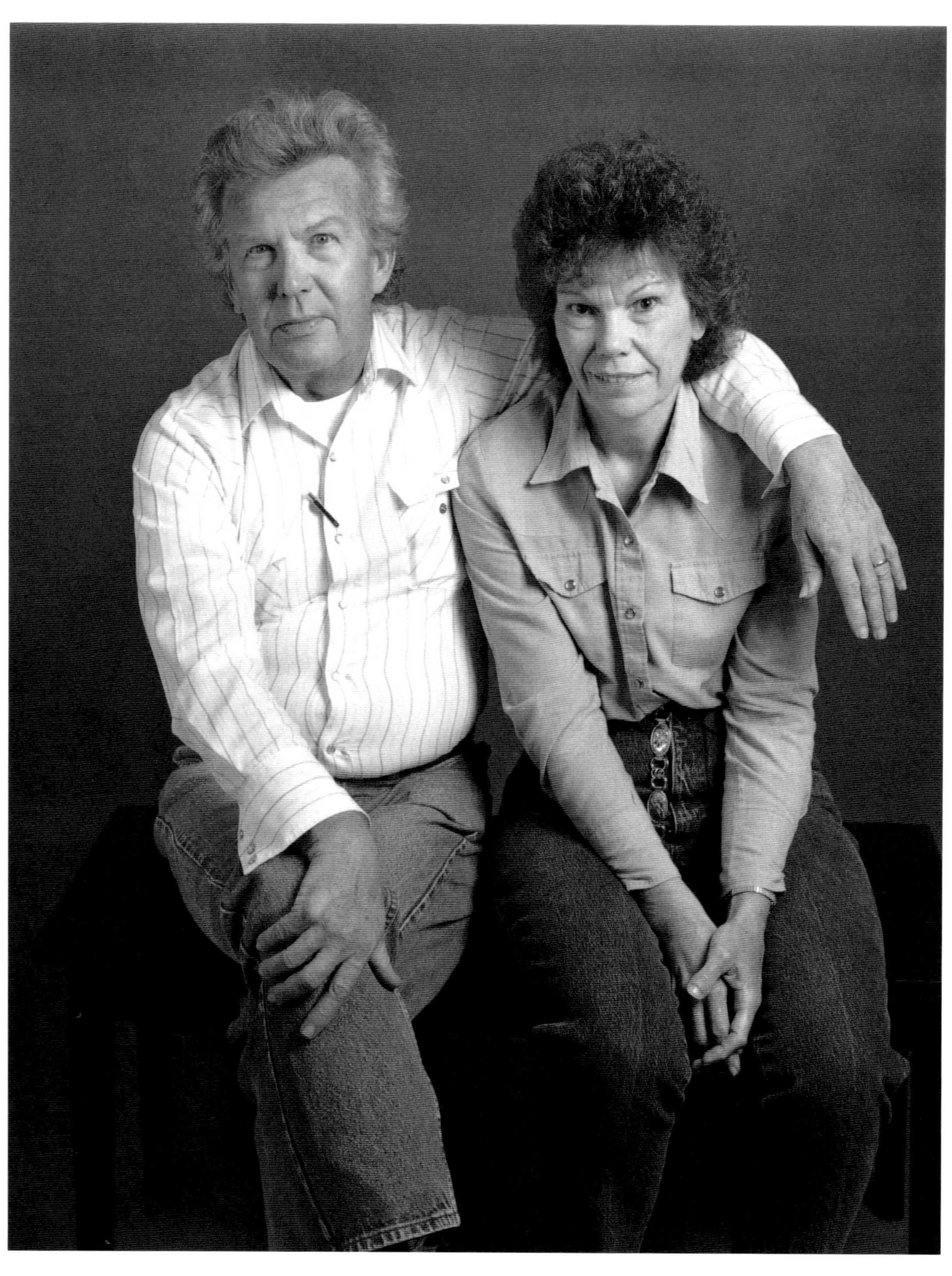

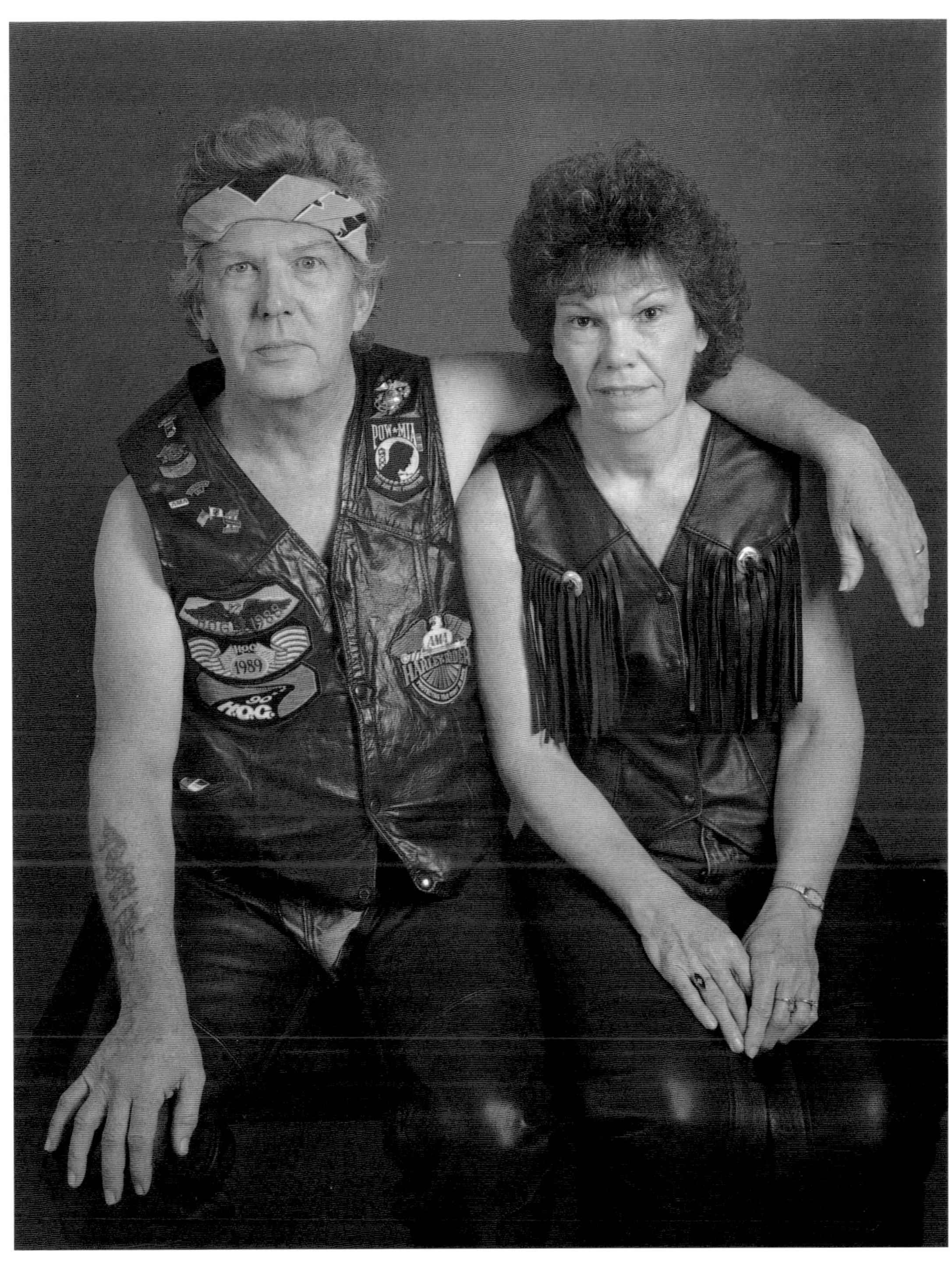
POW★MIA
1989
H.O.G.

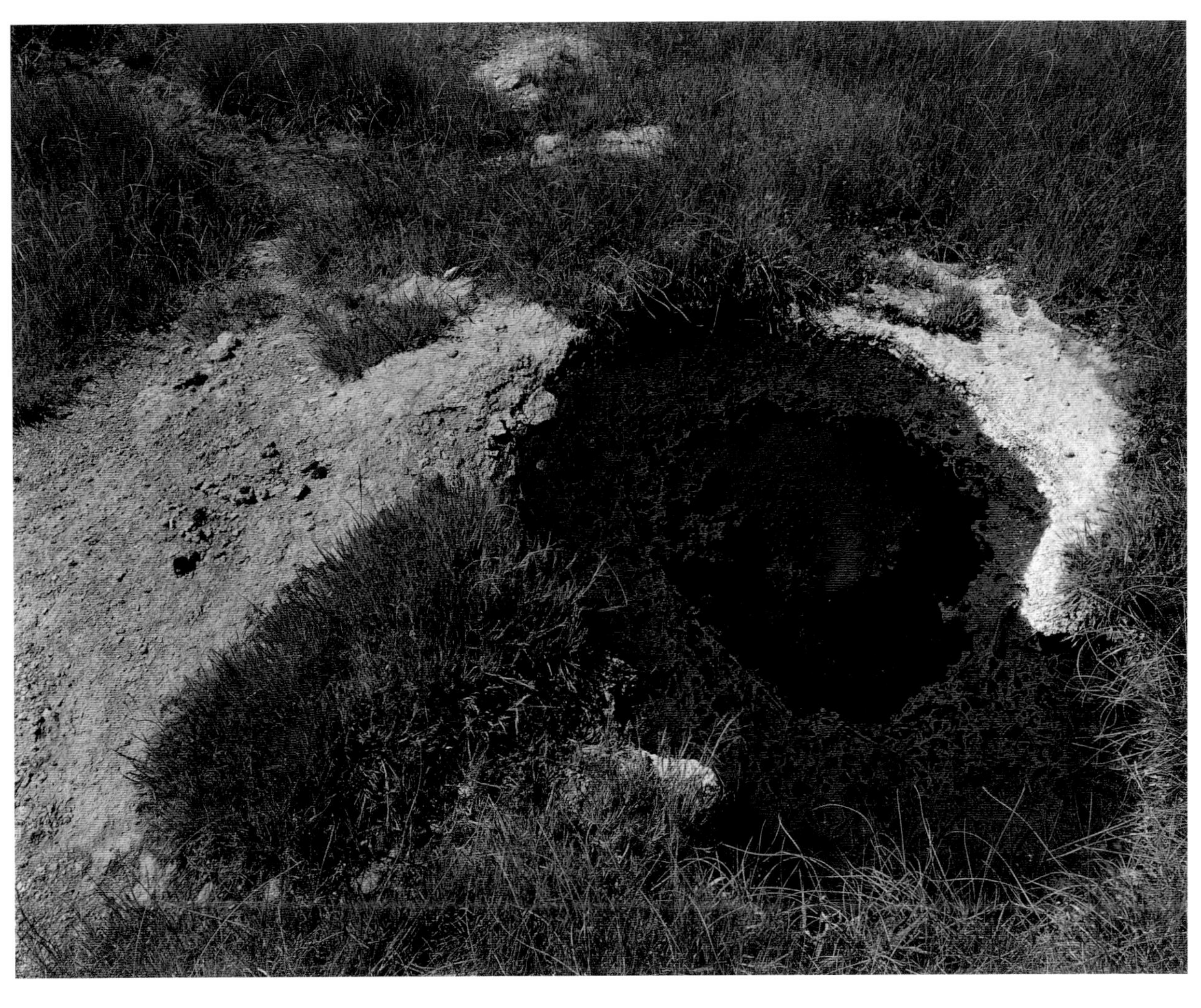

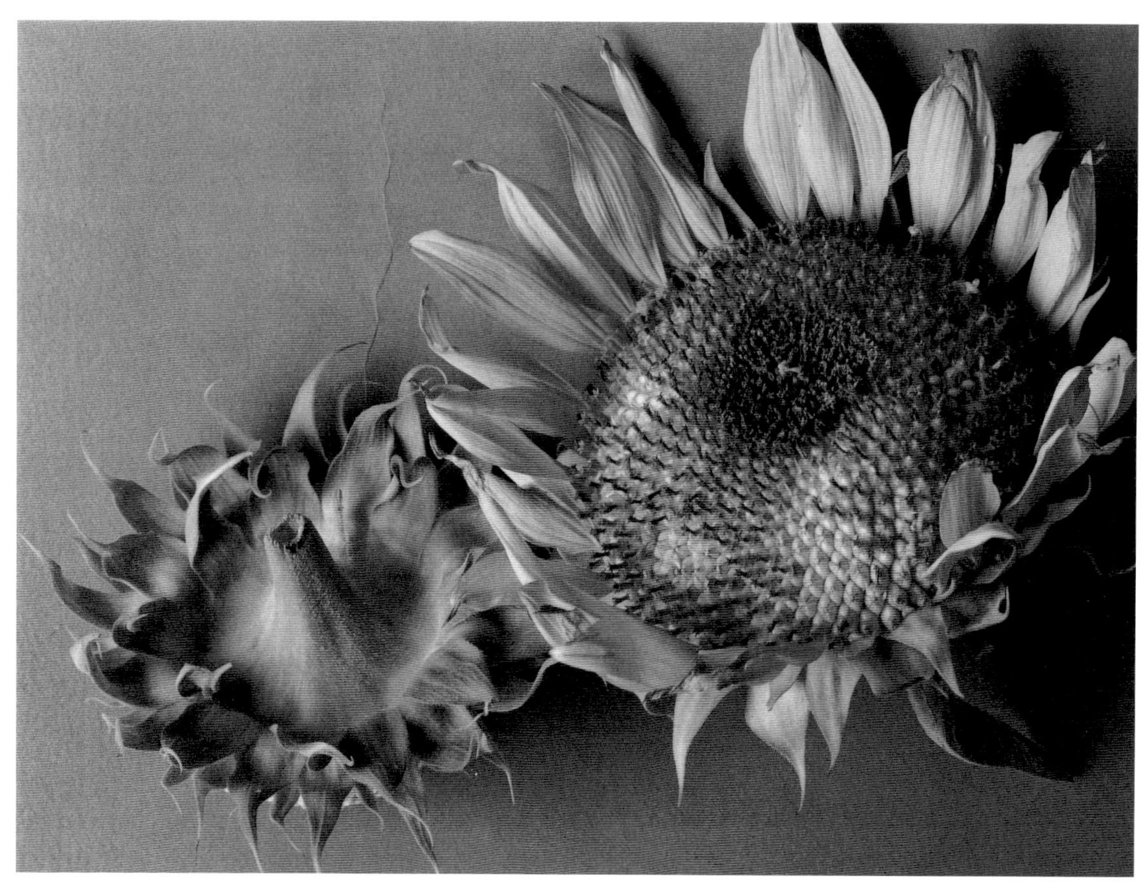

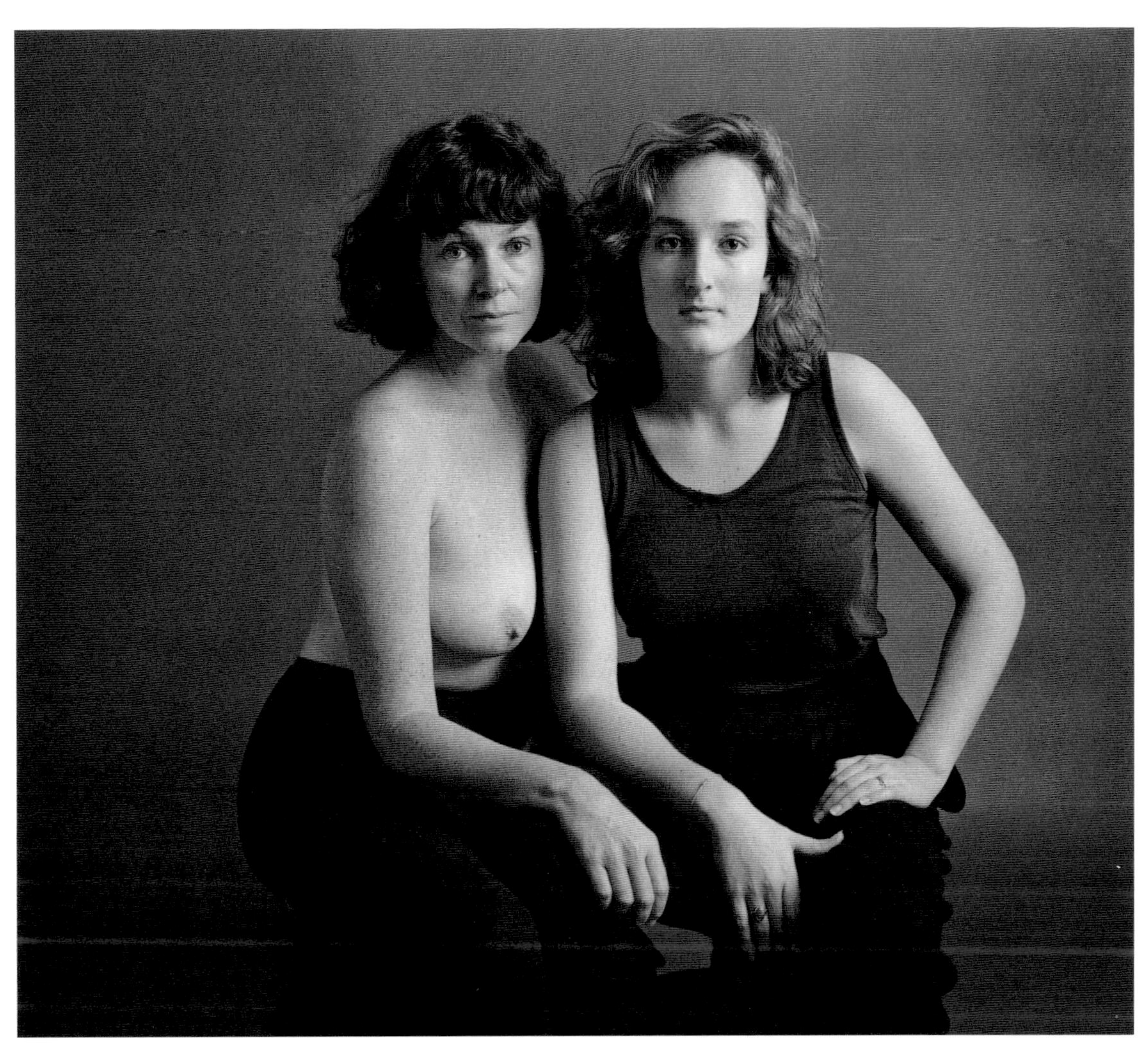

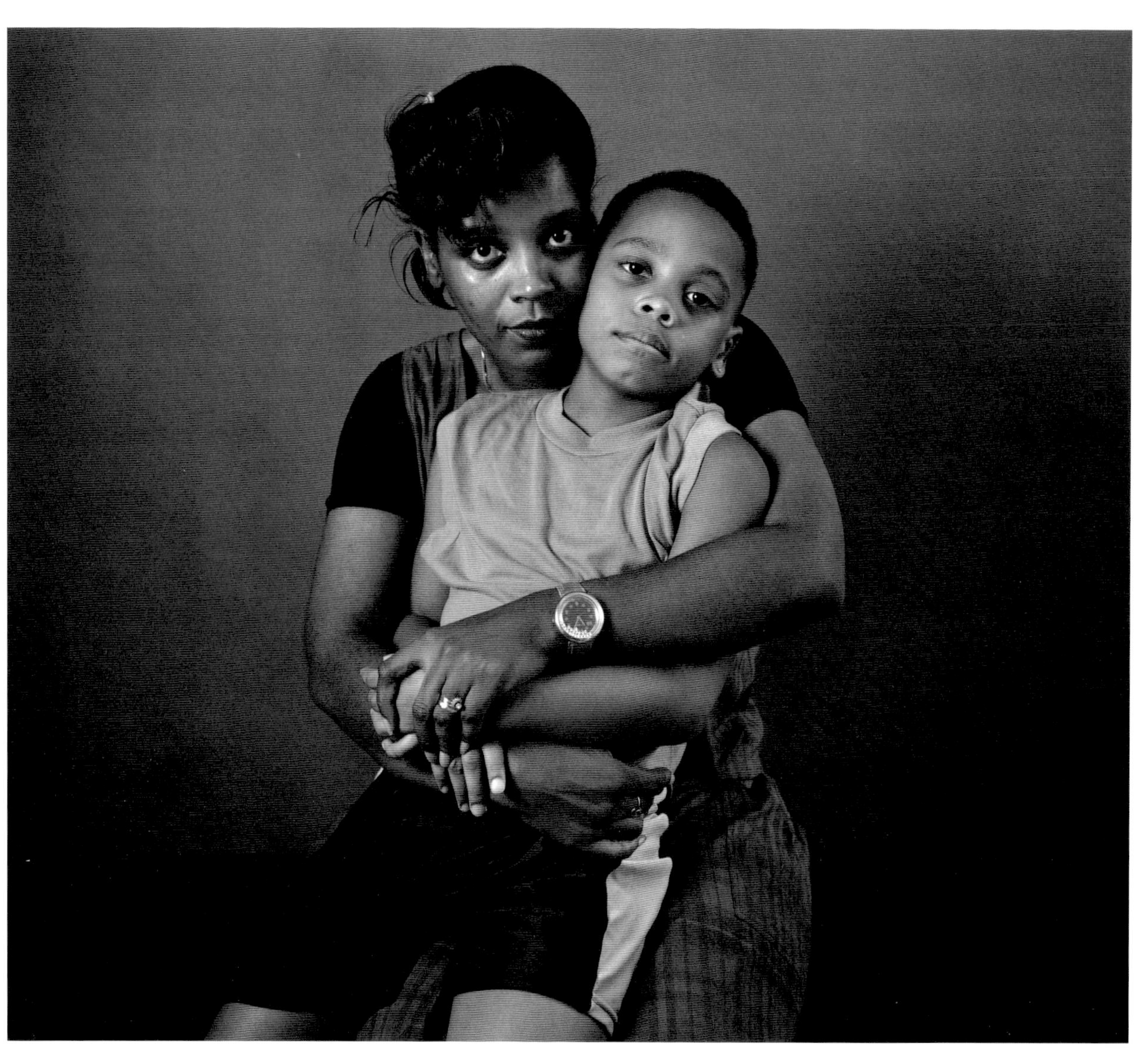

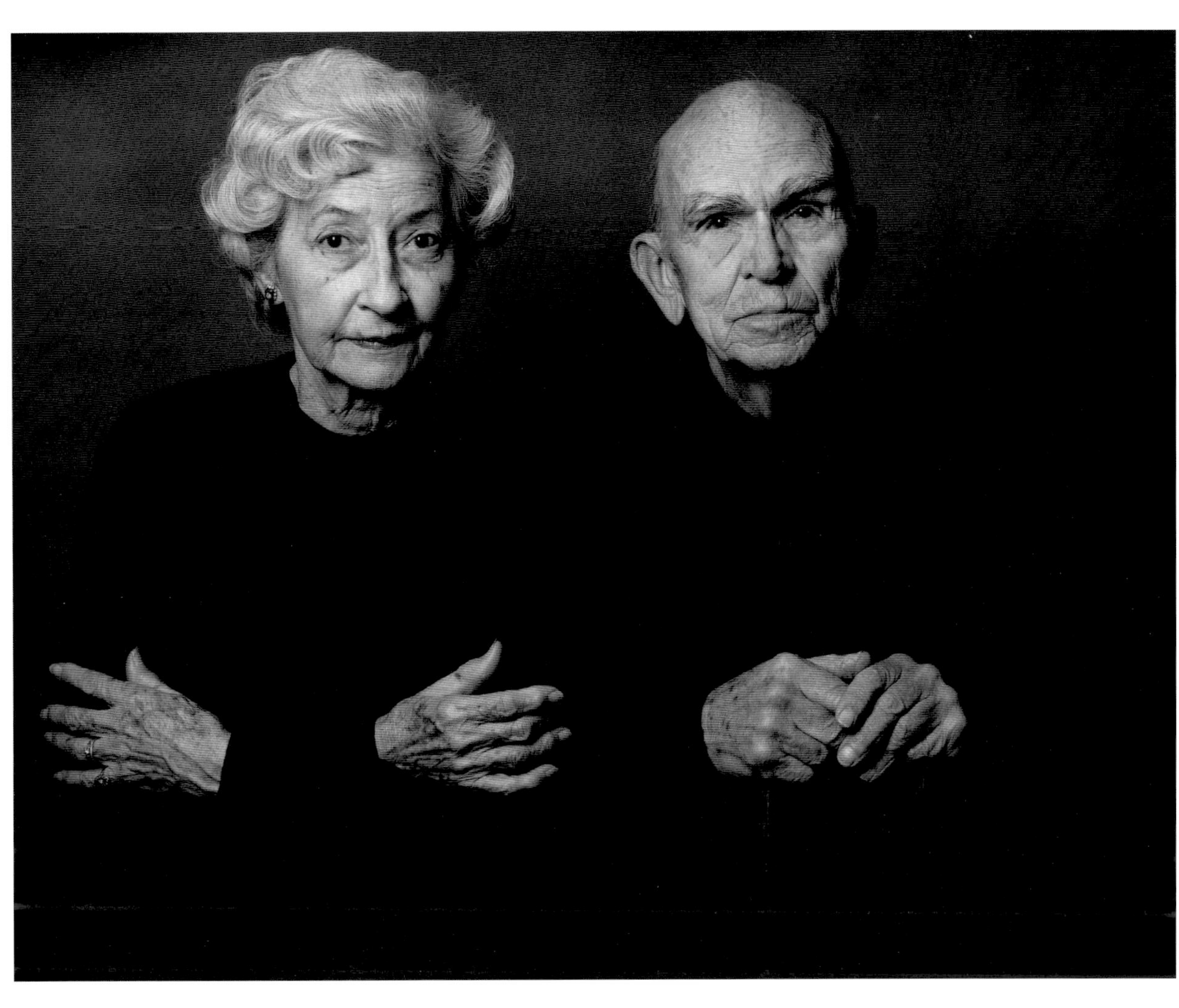

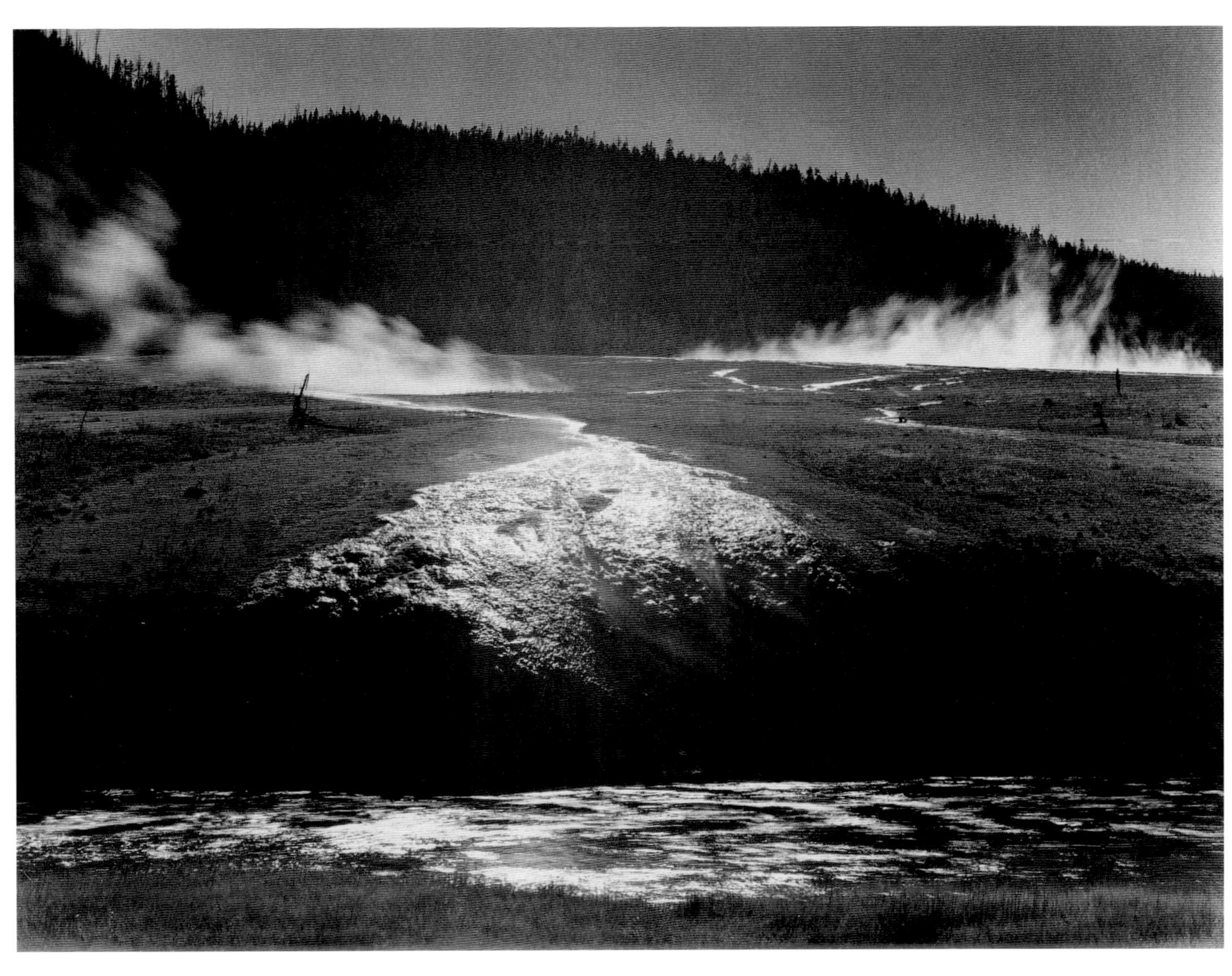

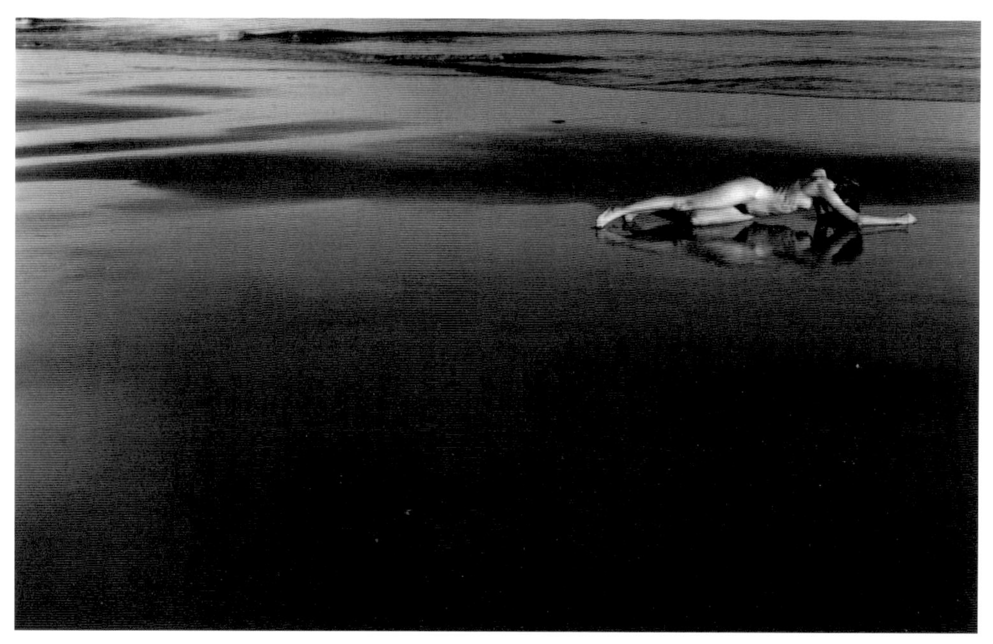

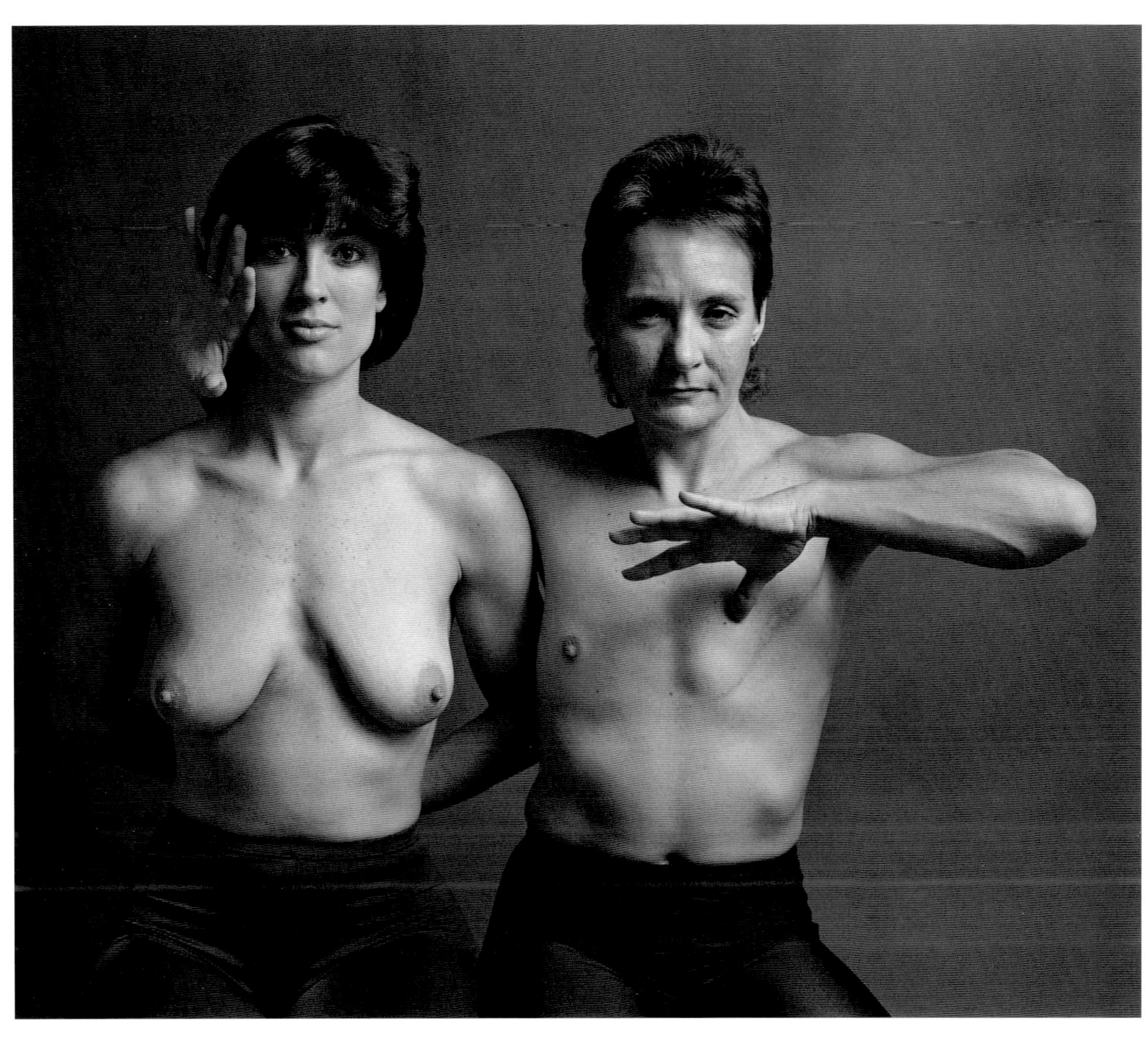

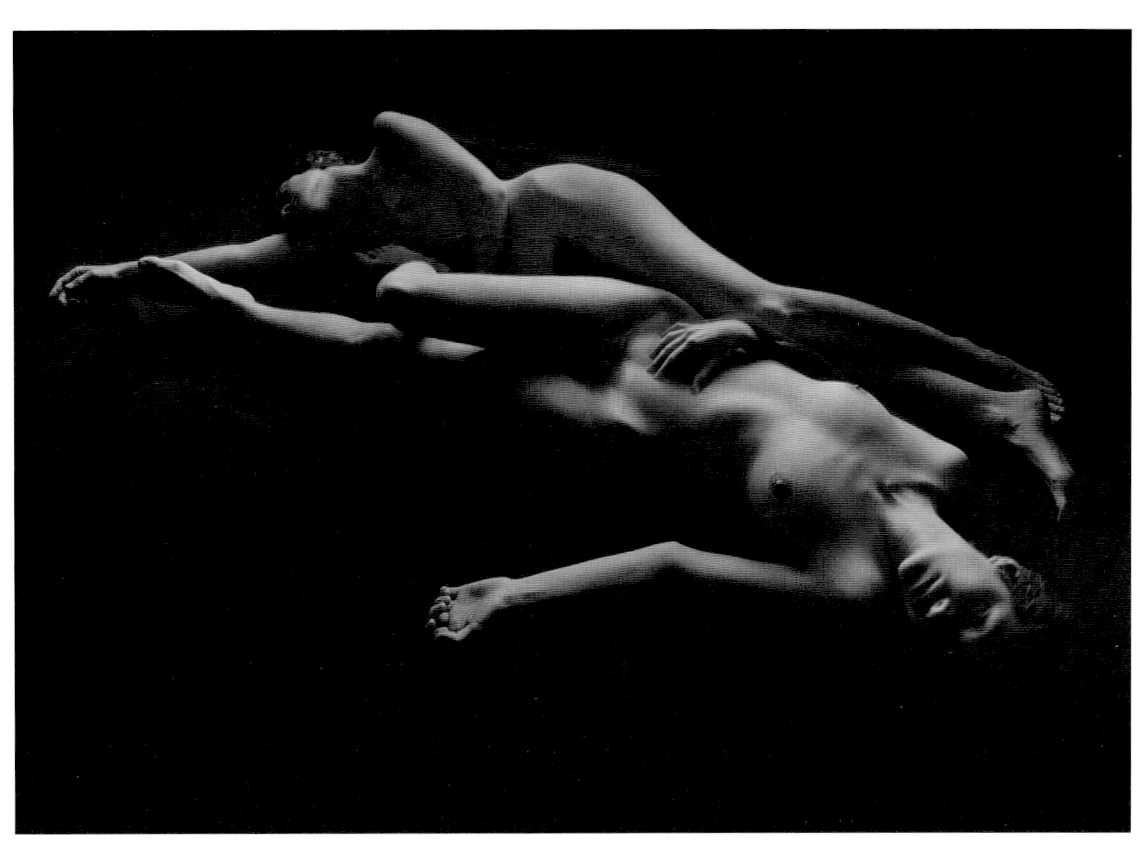

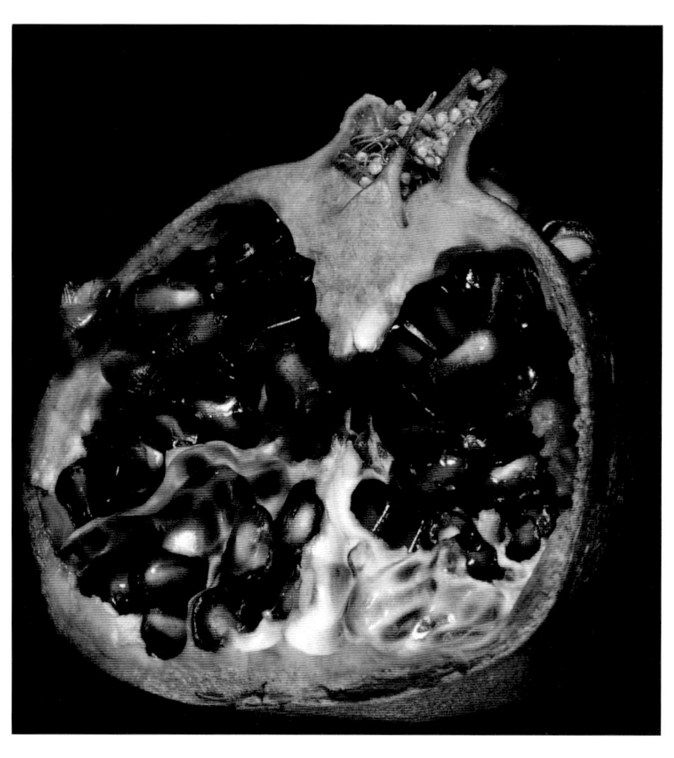

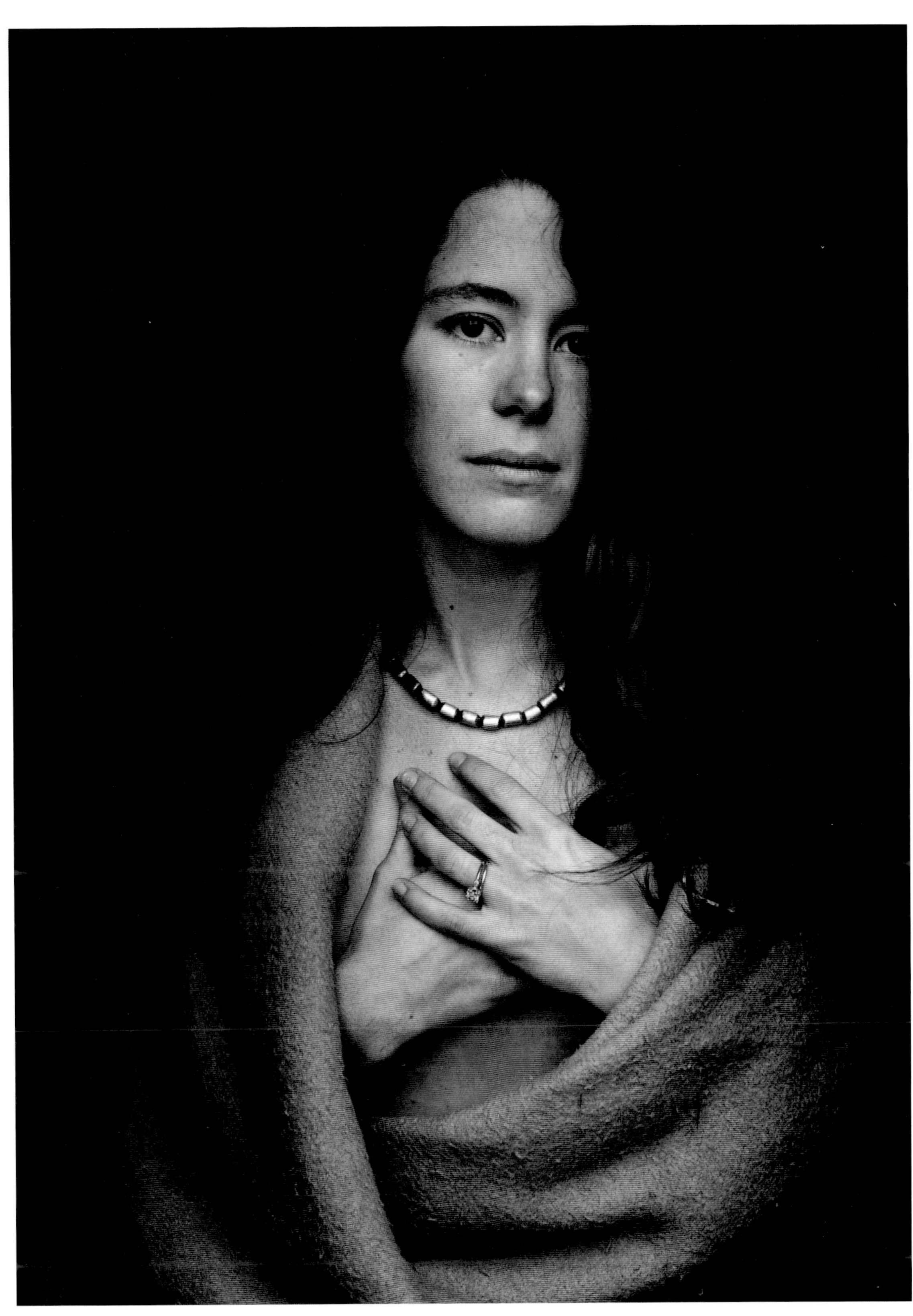

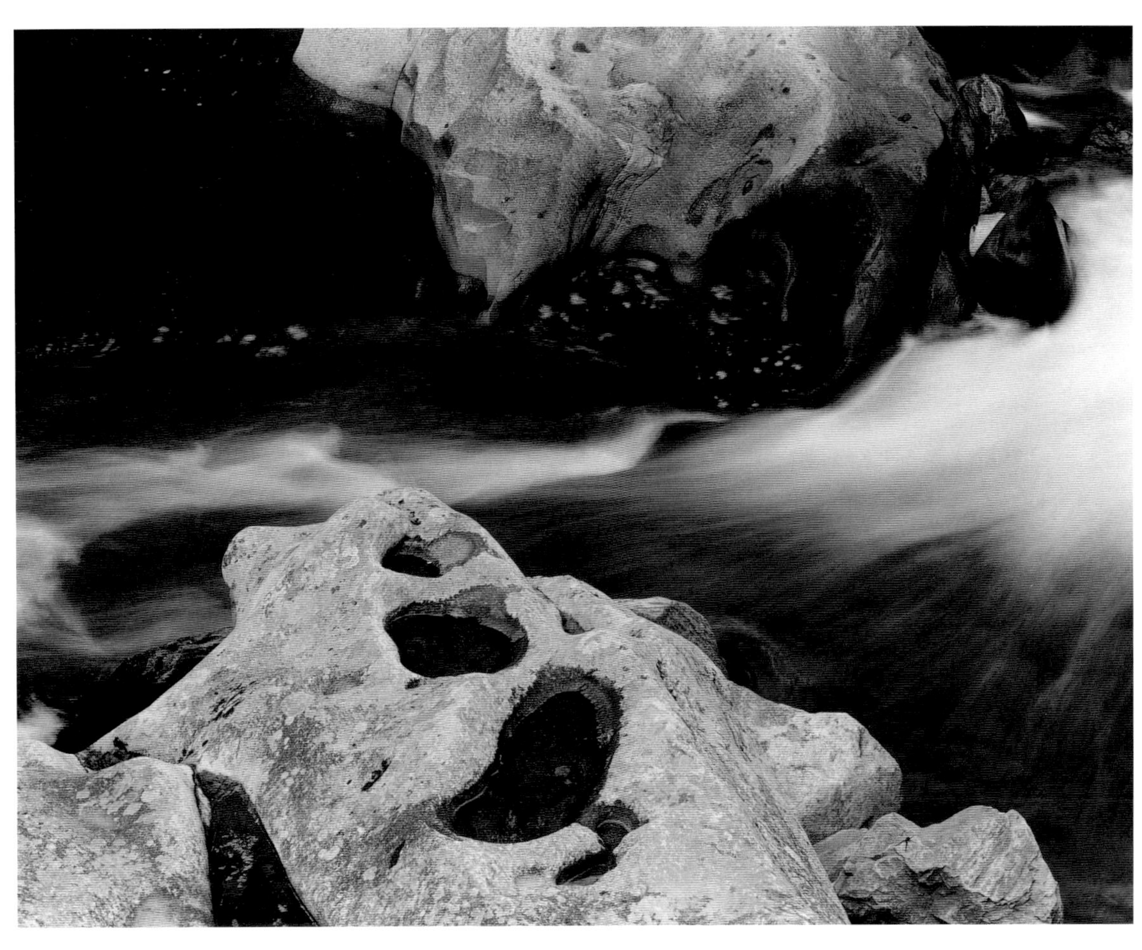

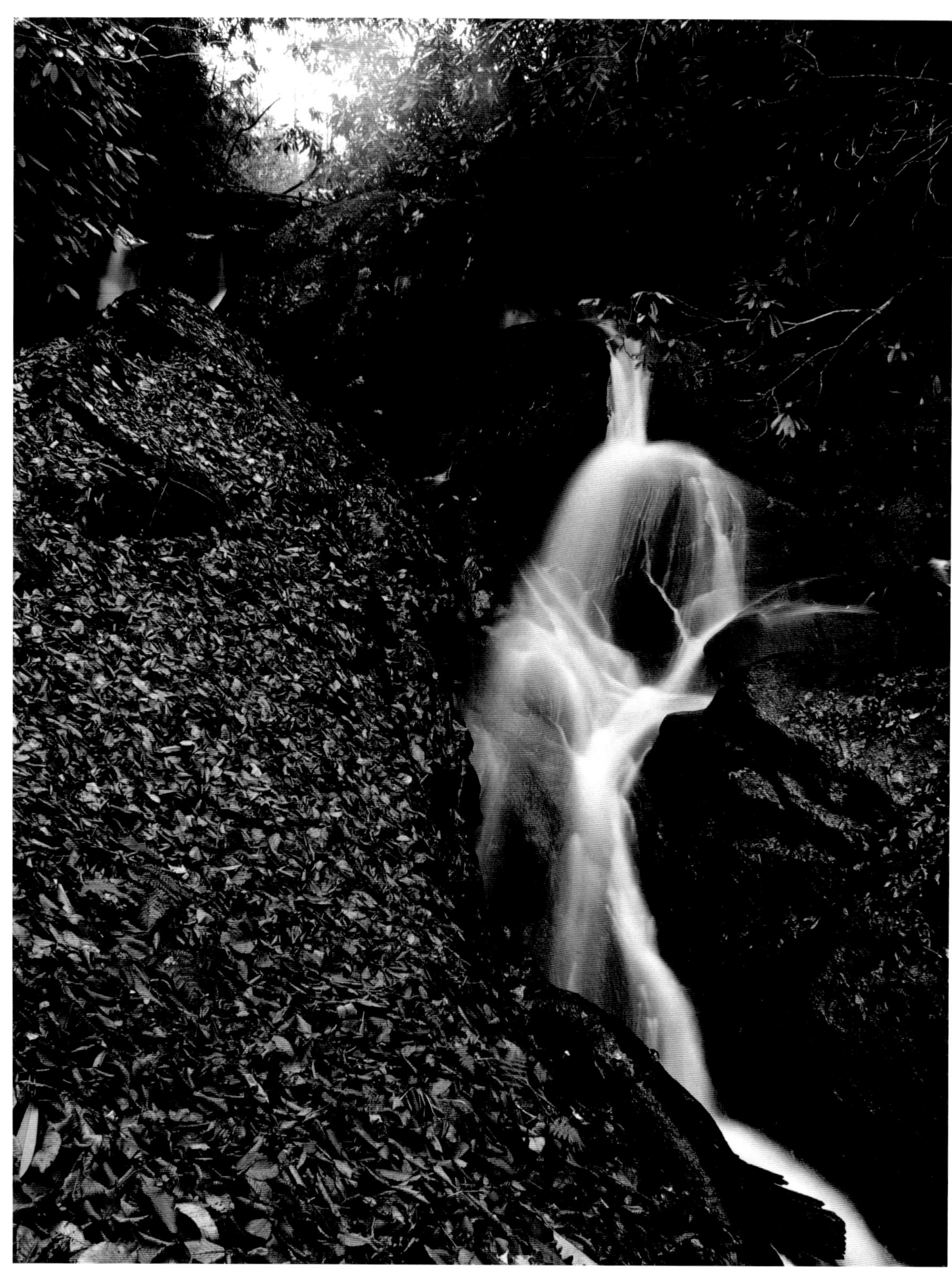

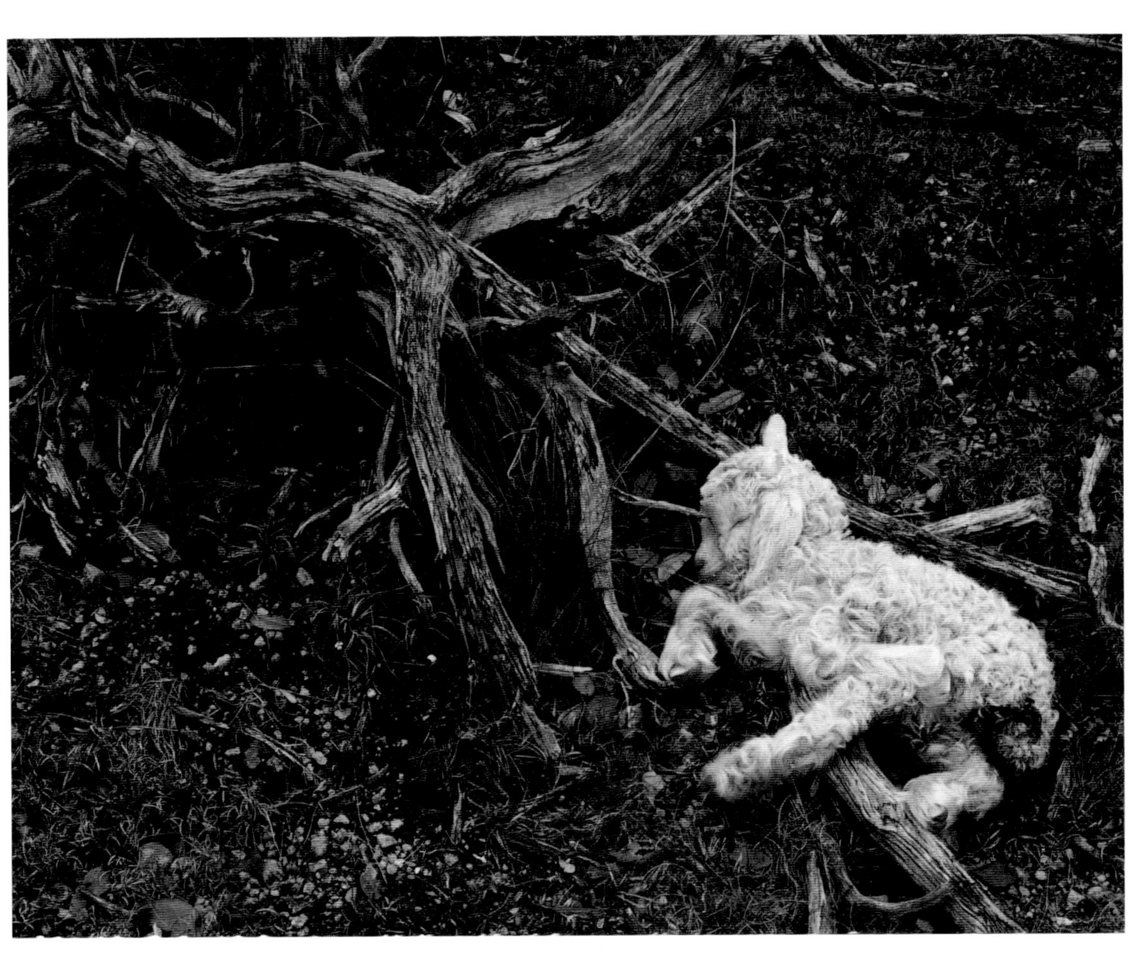

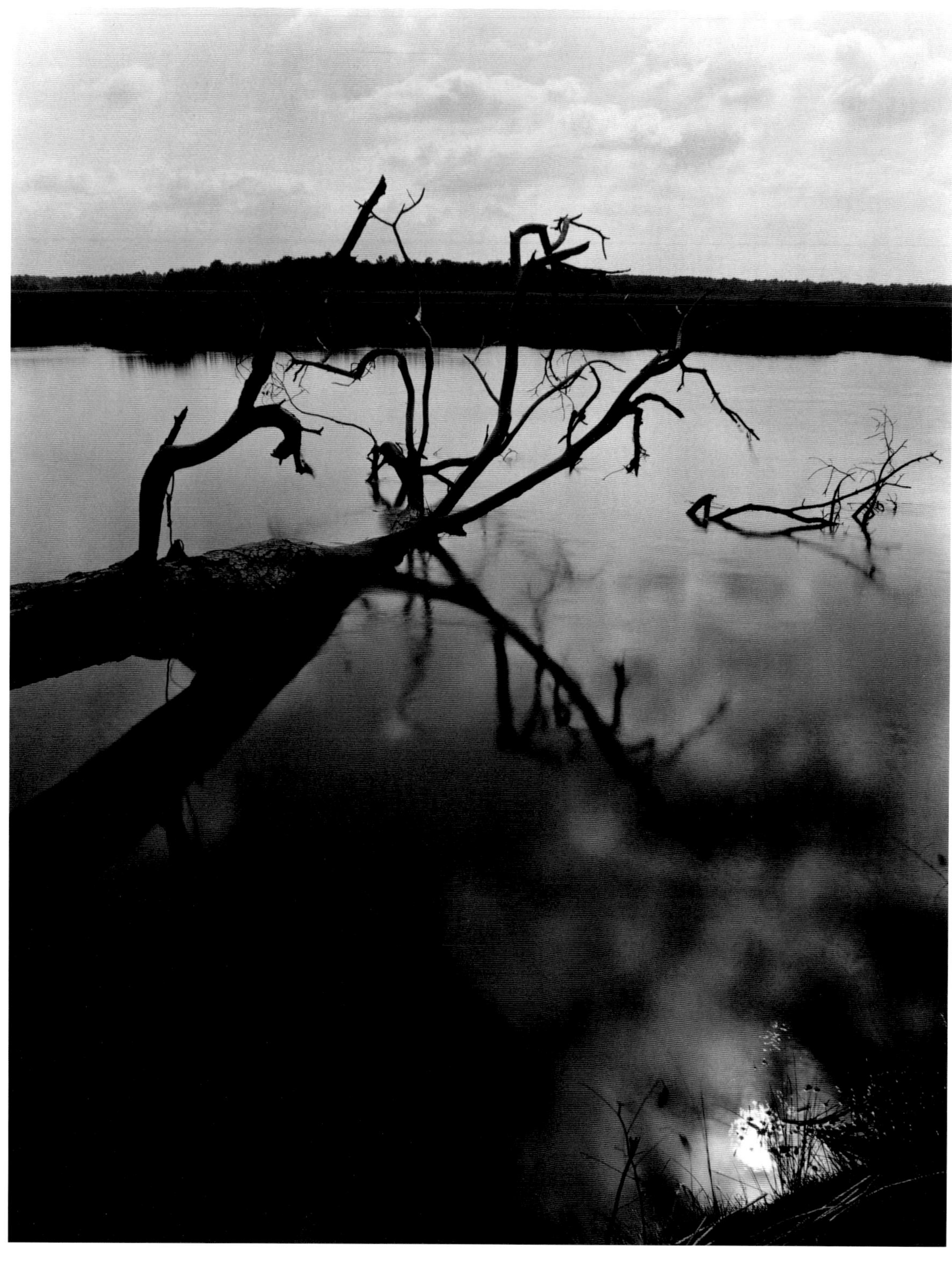

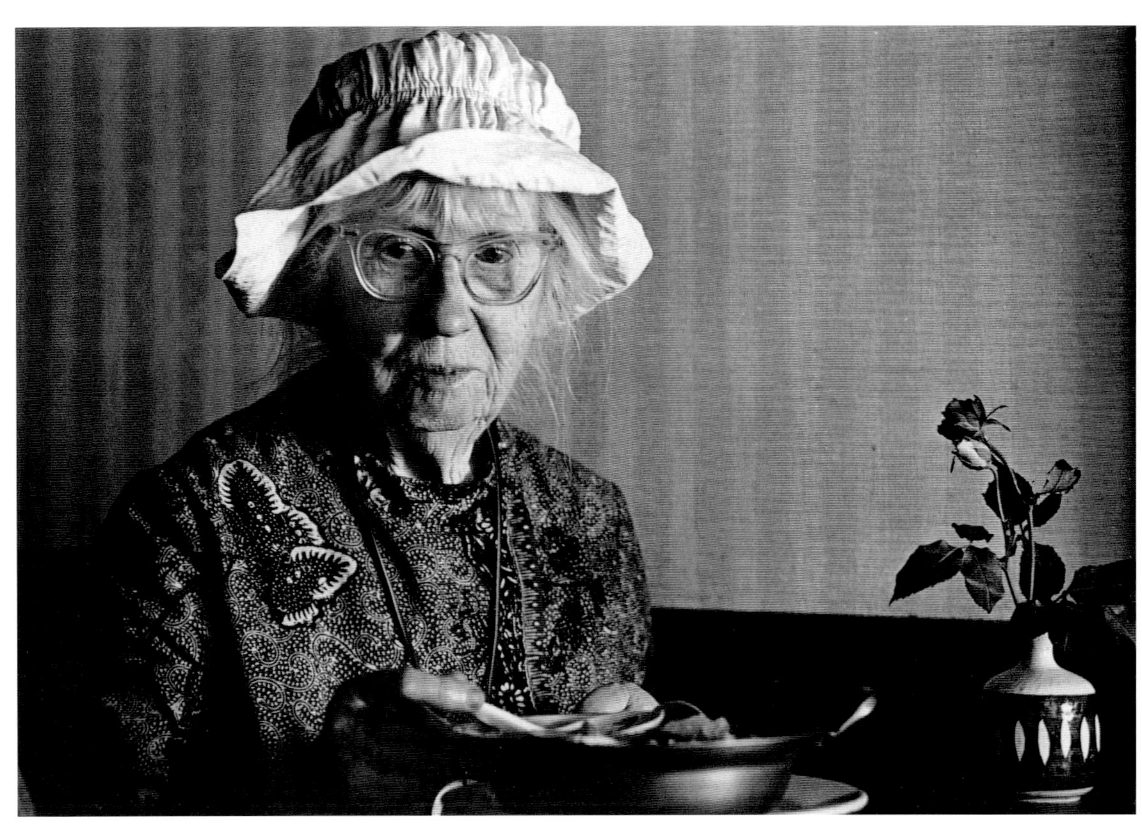

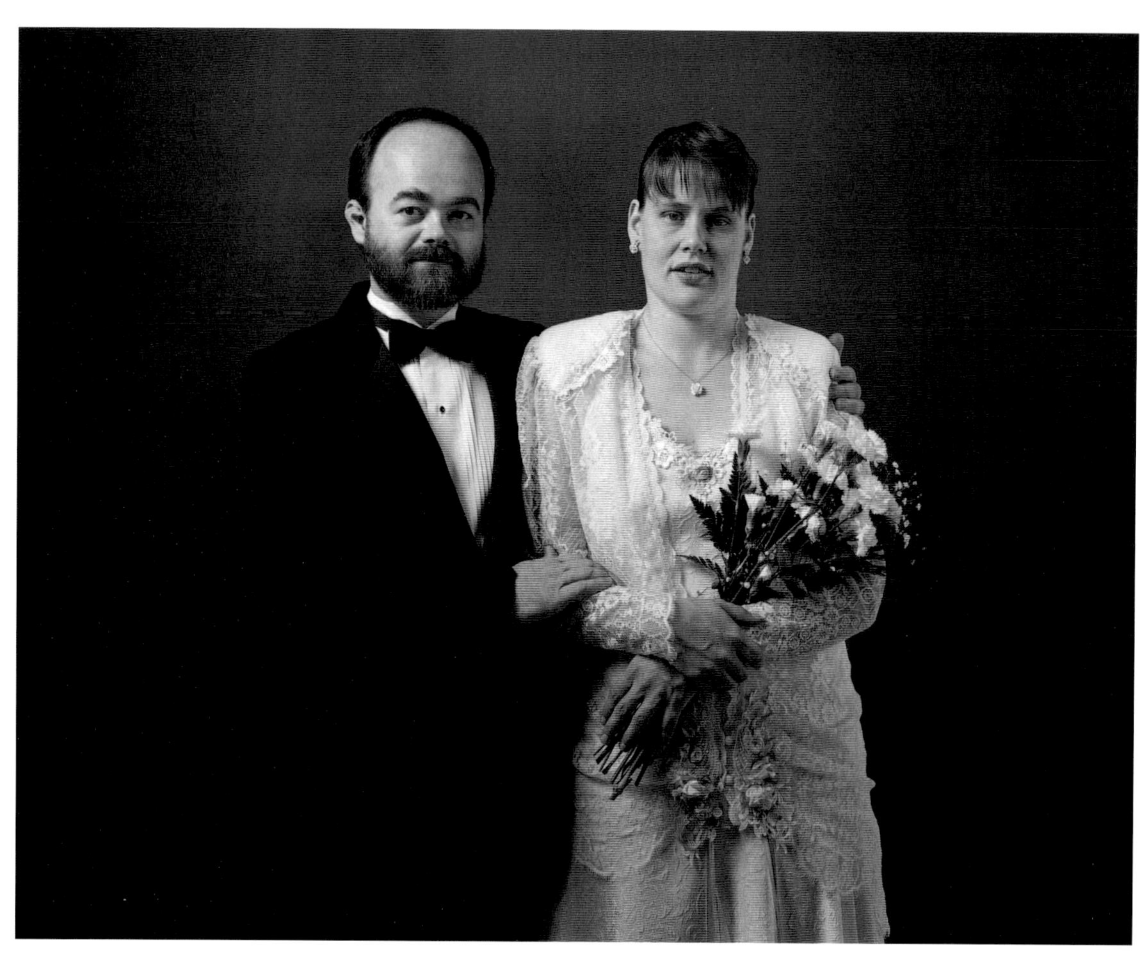

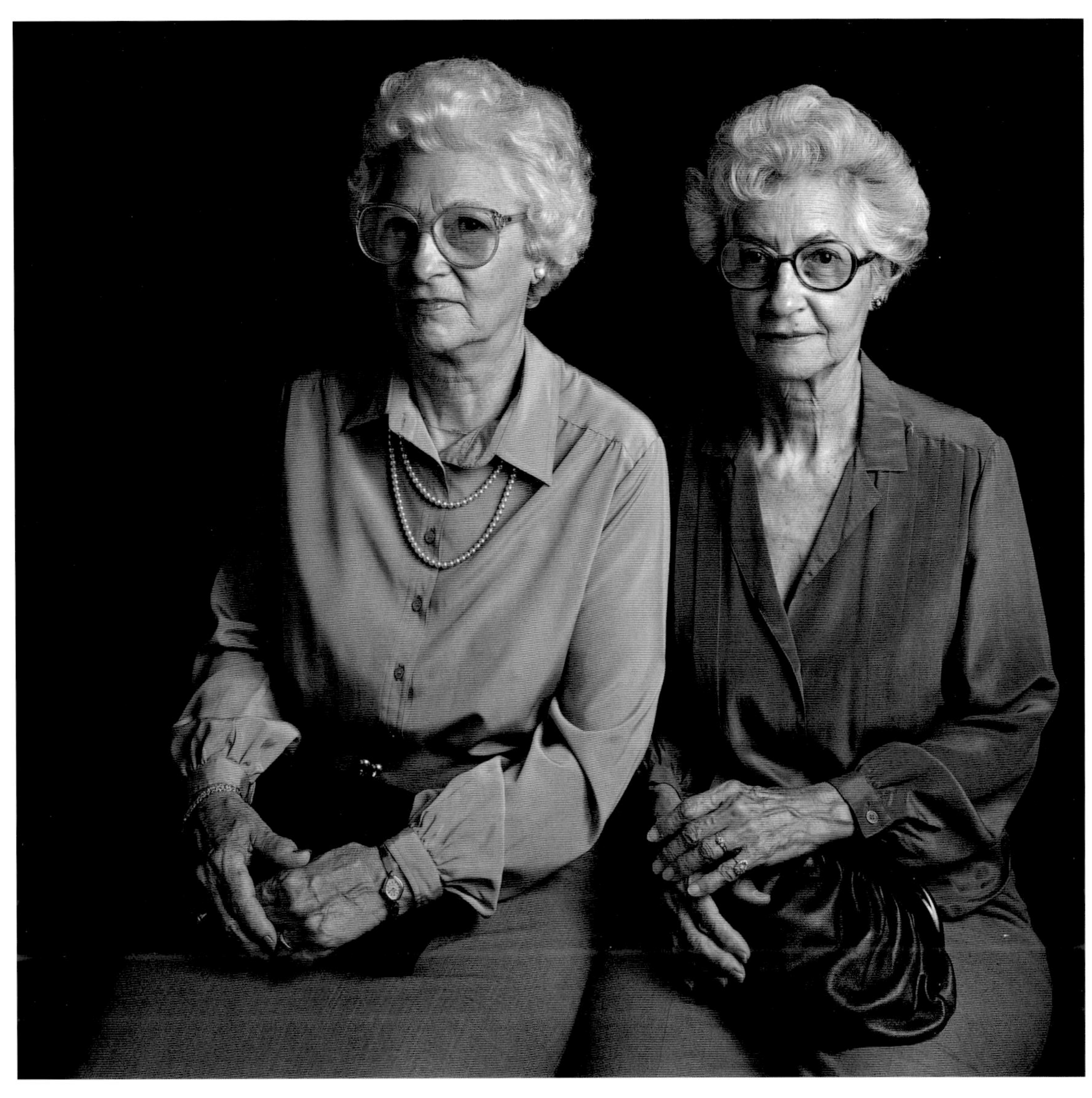

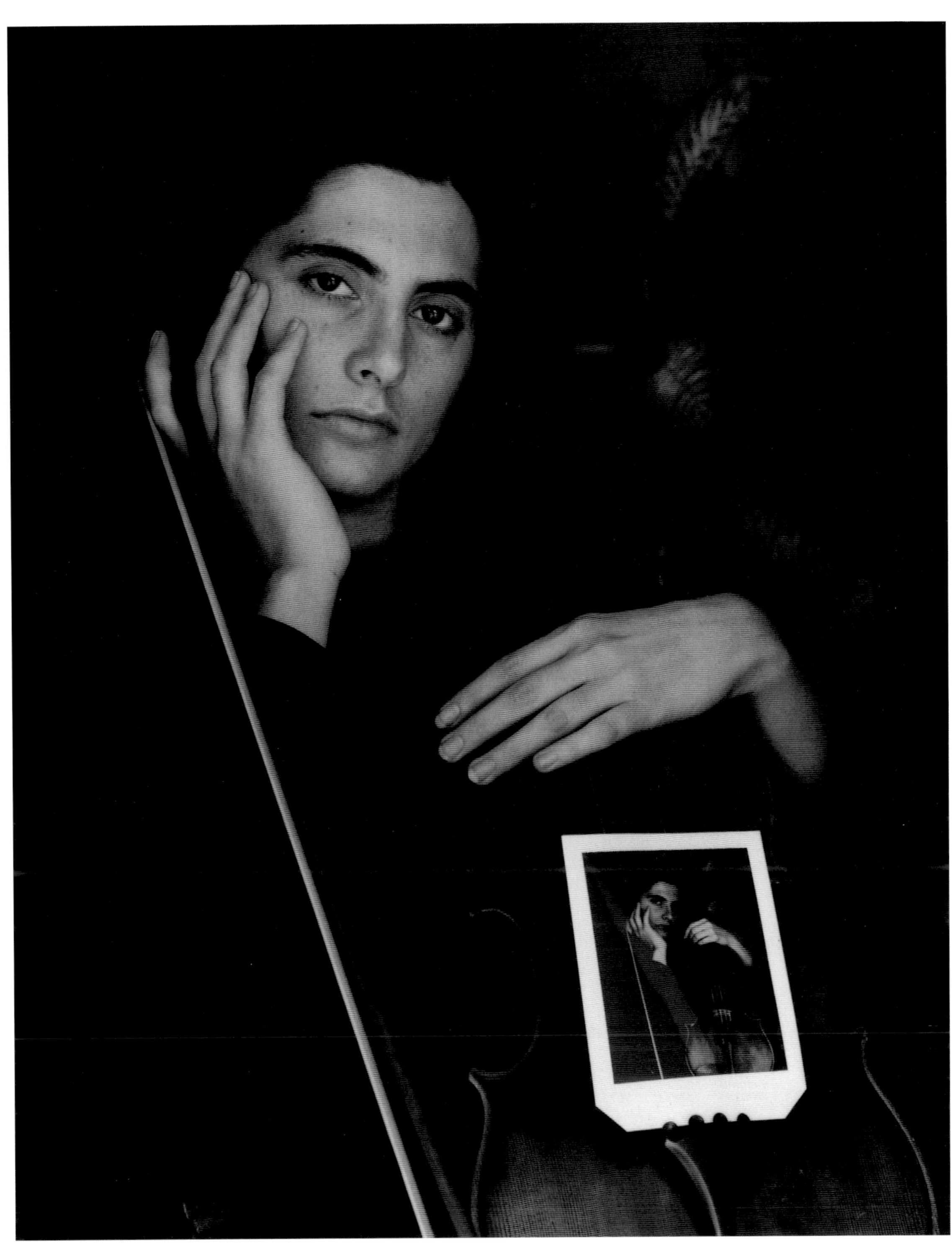

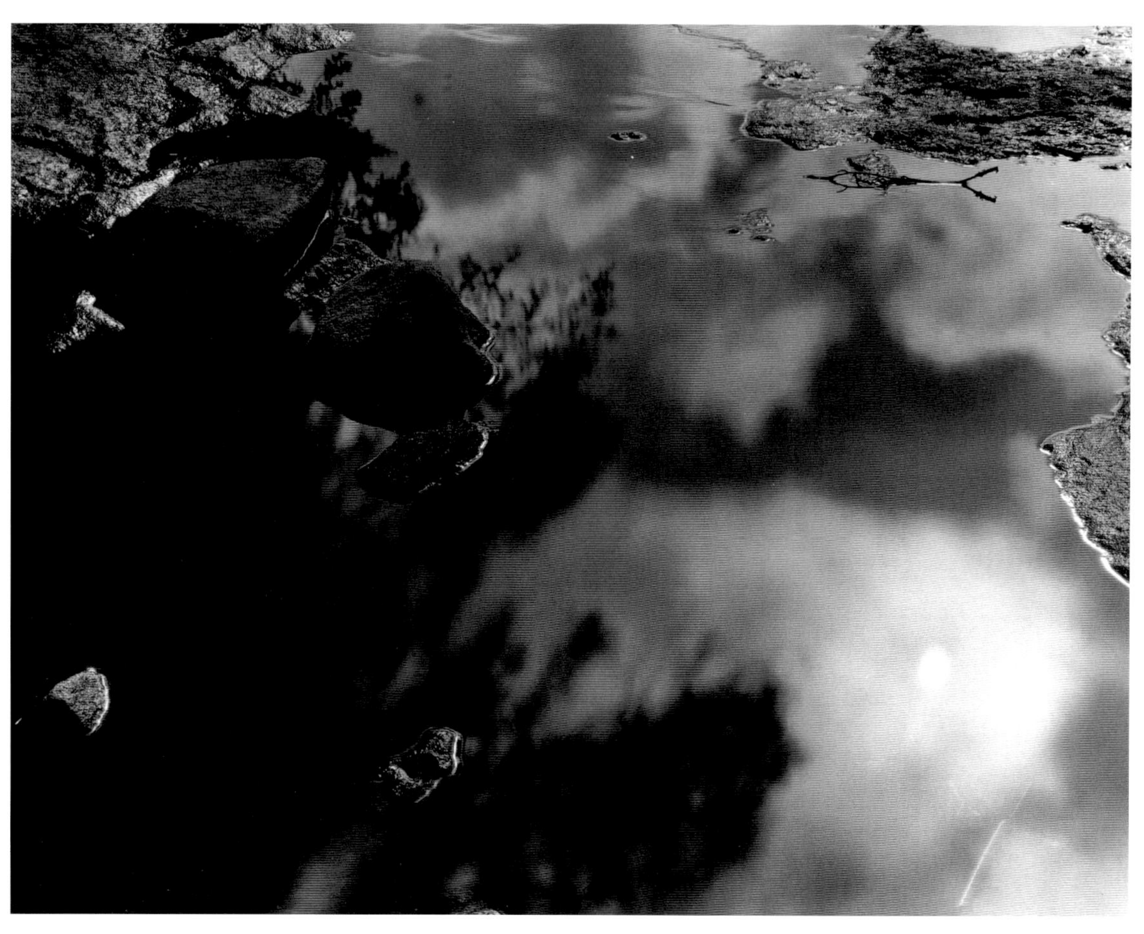

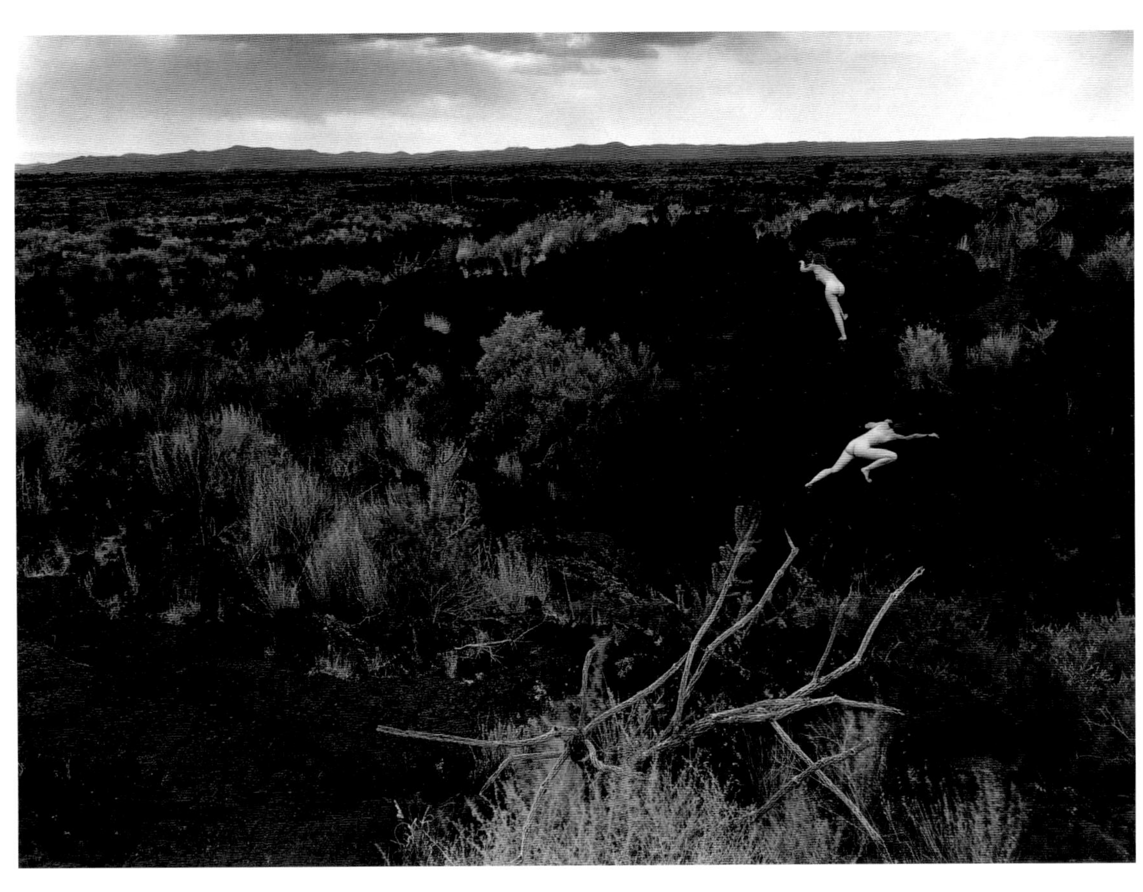

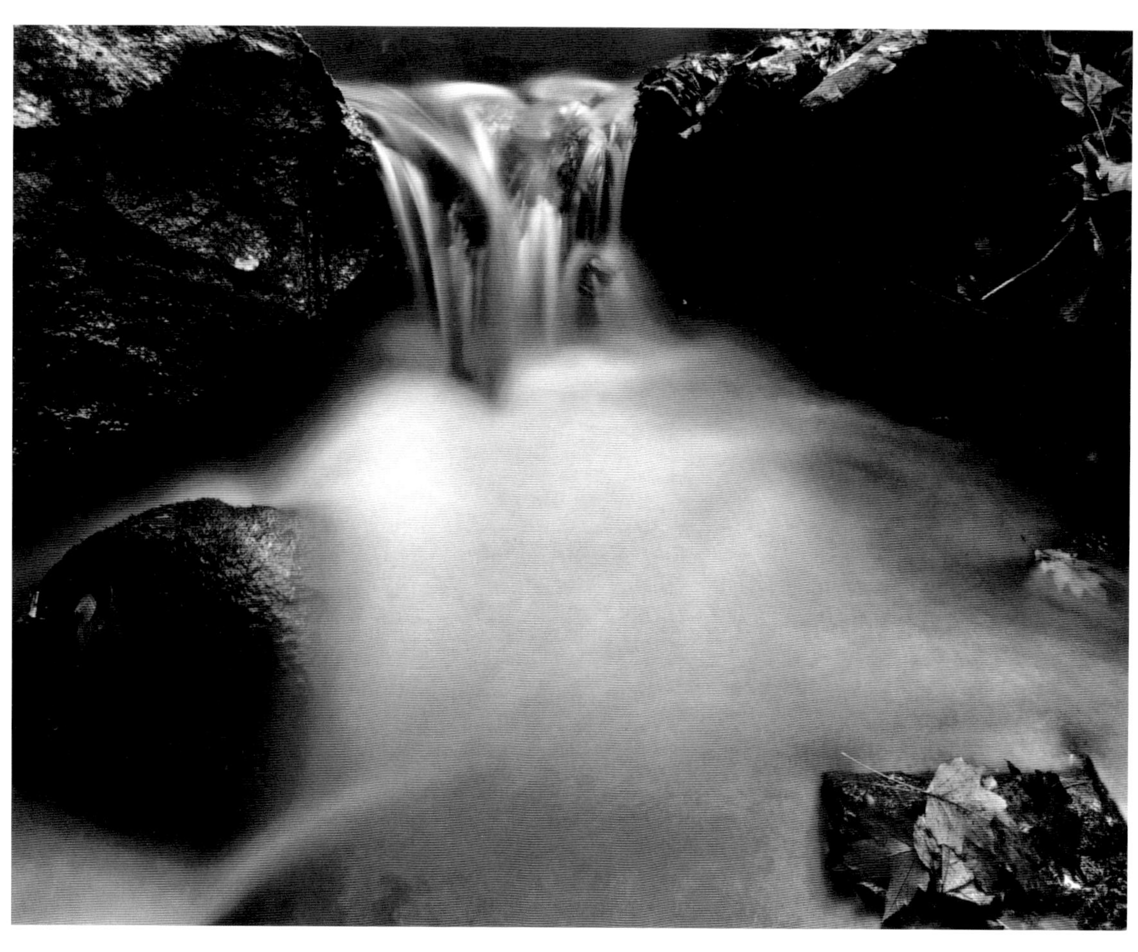

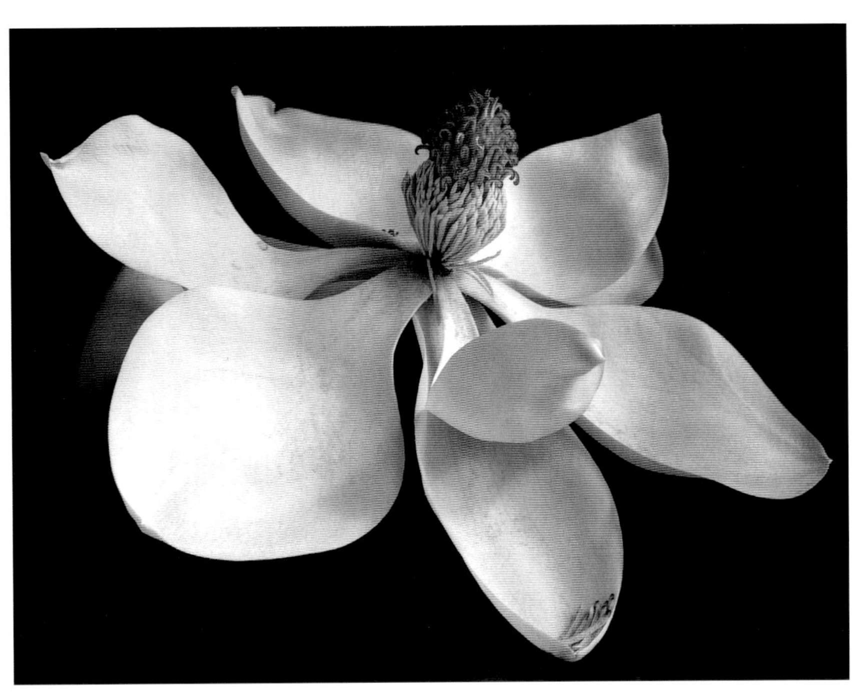

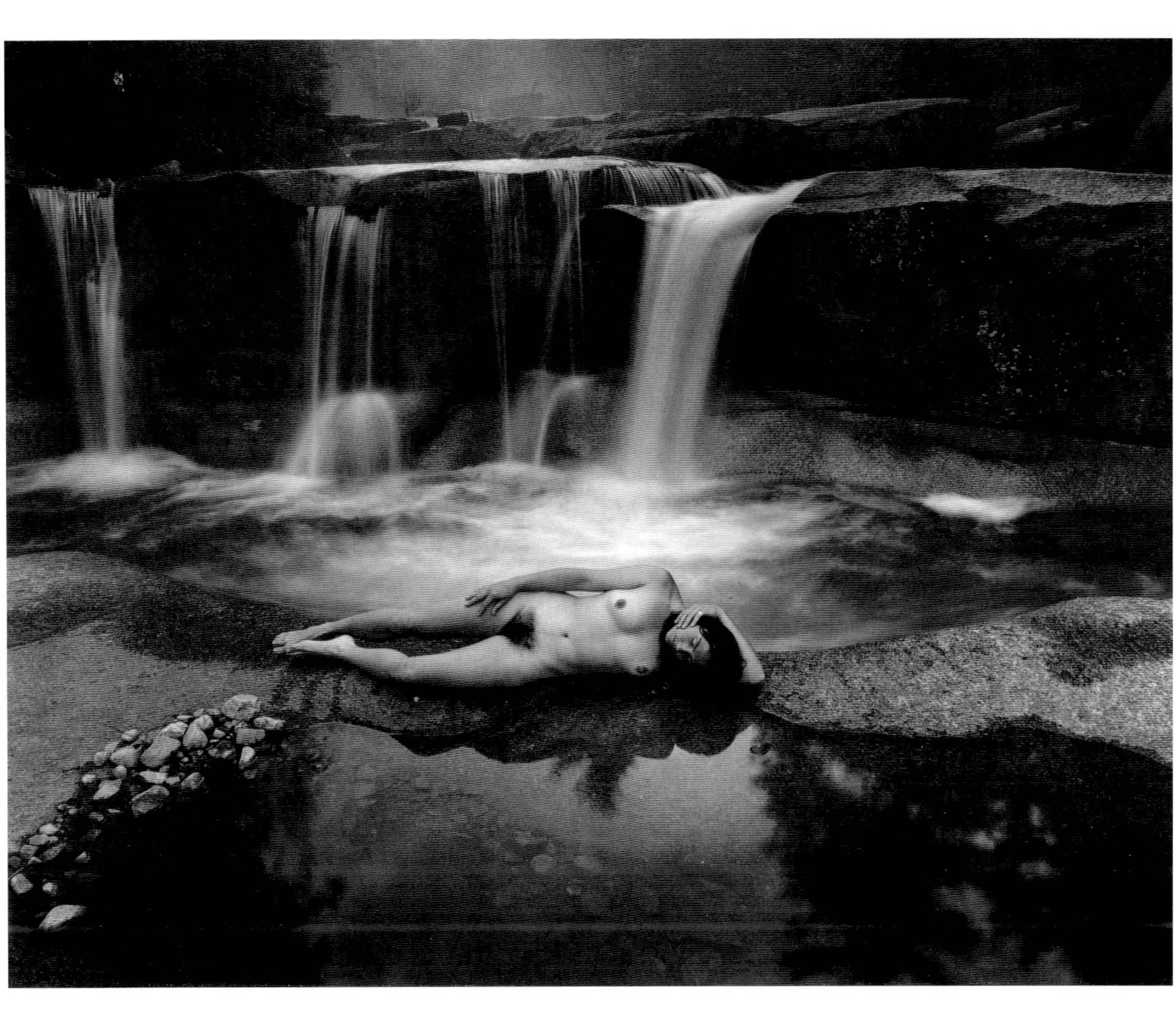

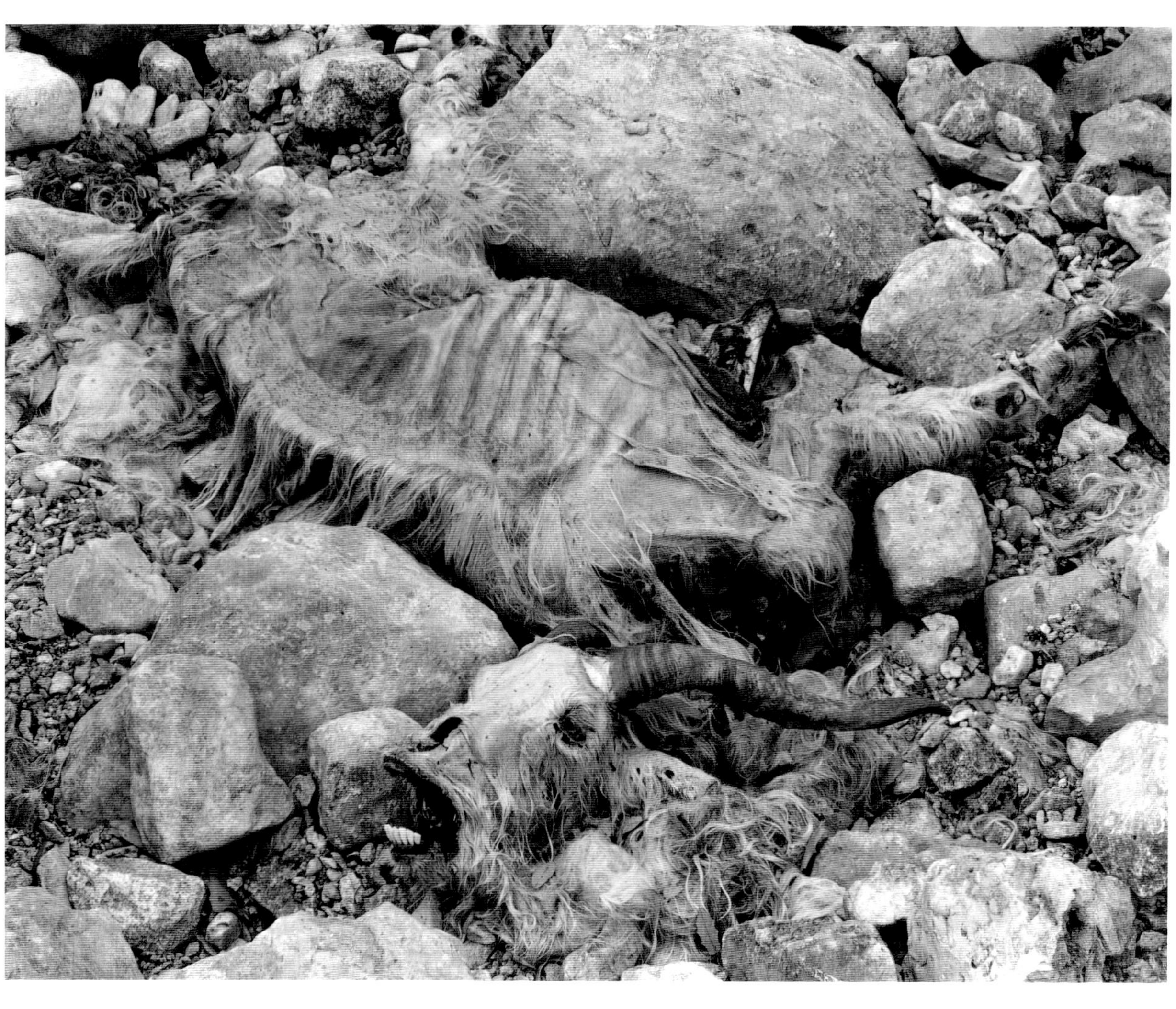

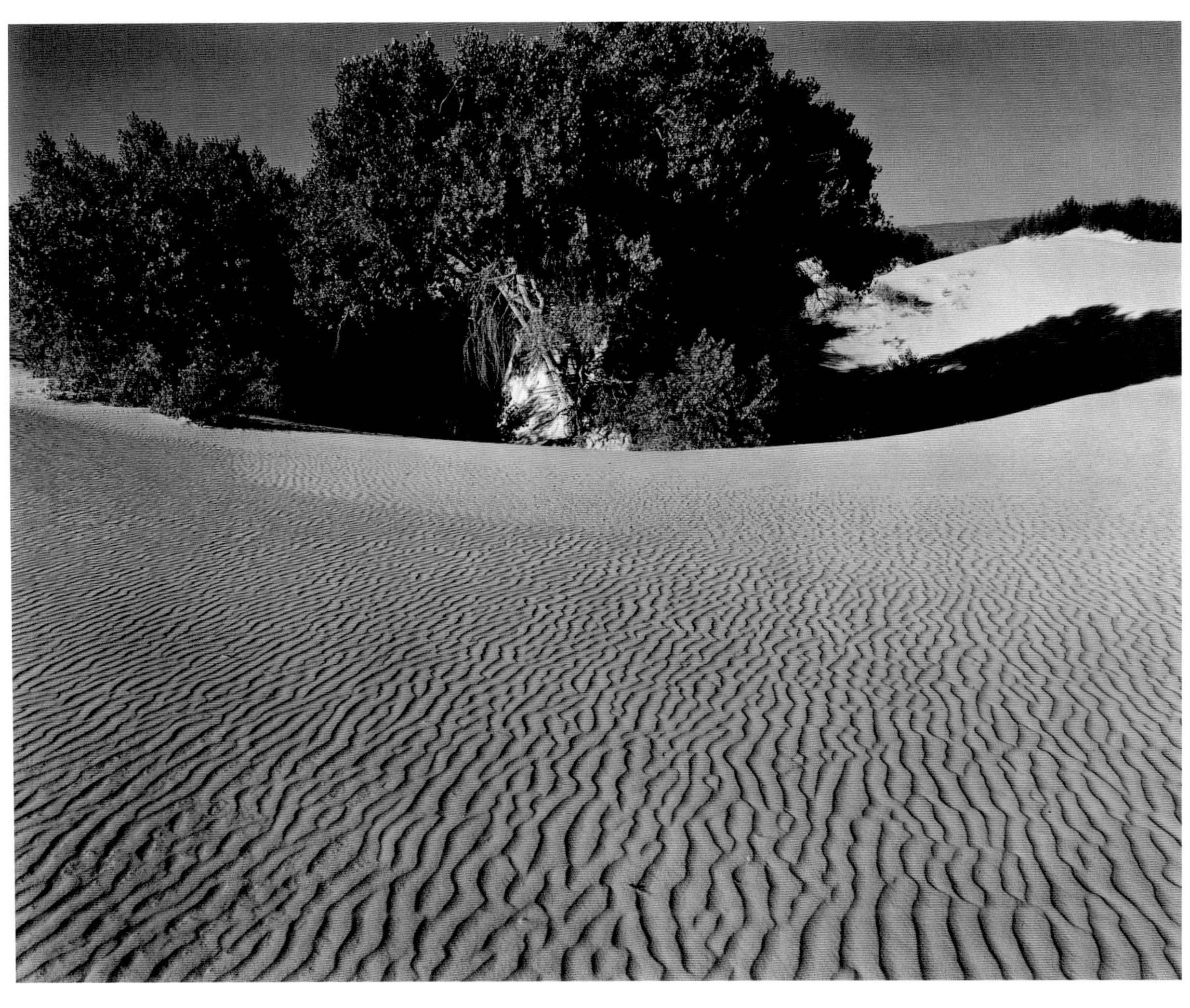

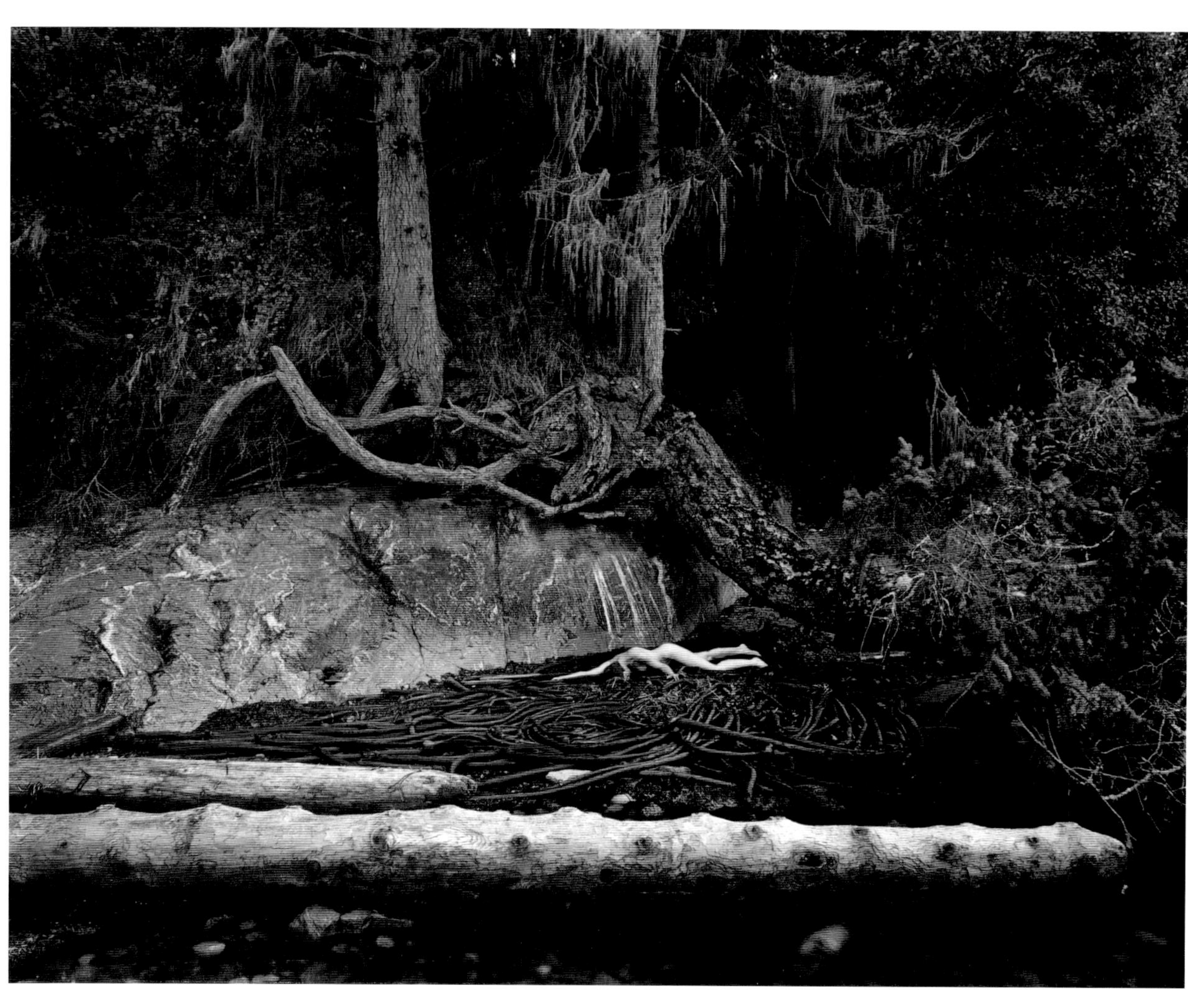

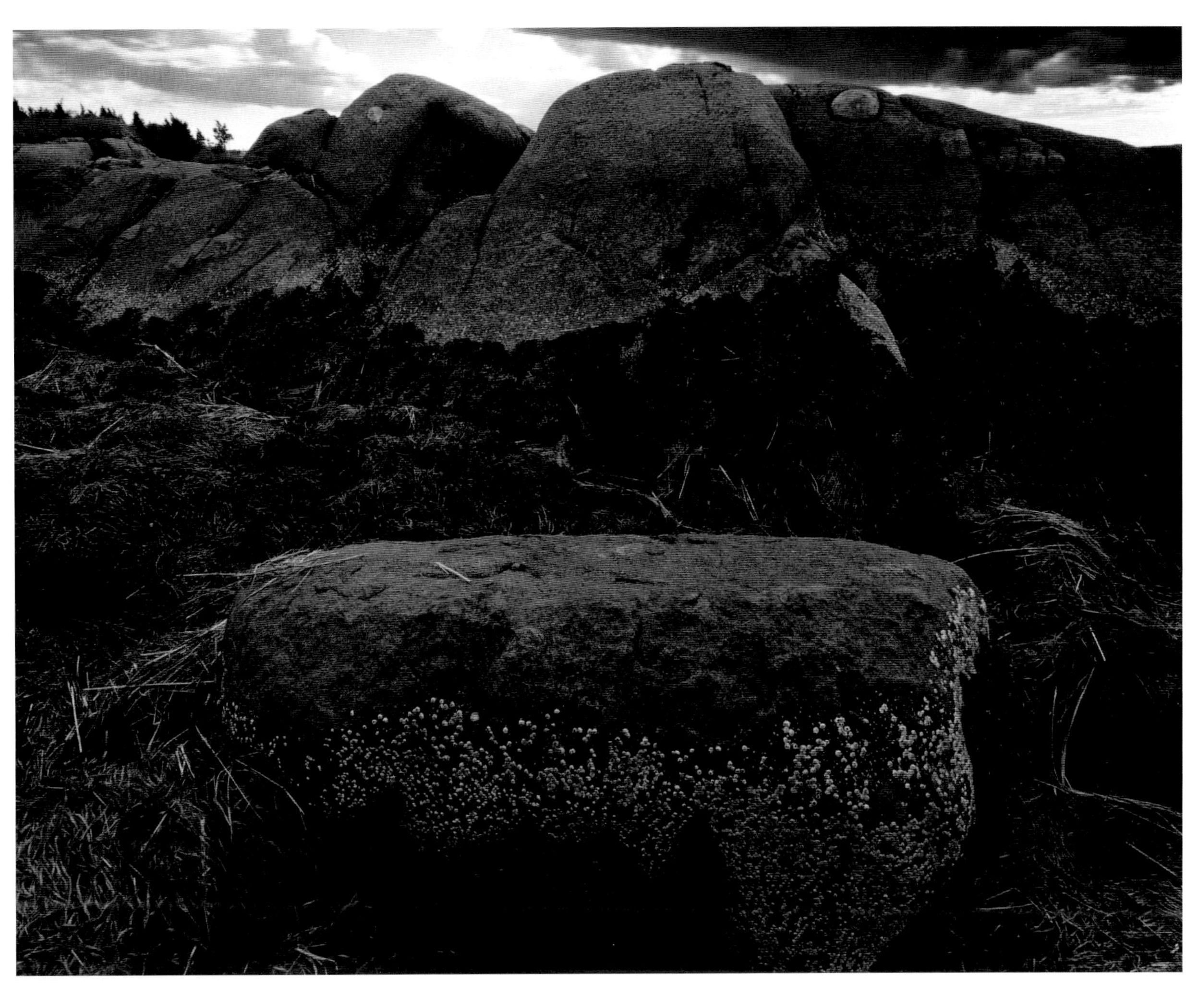

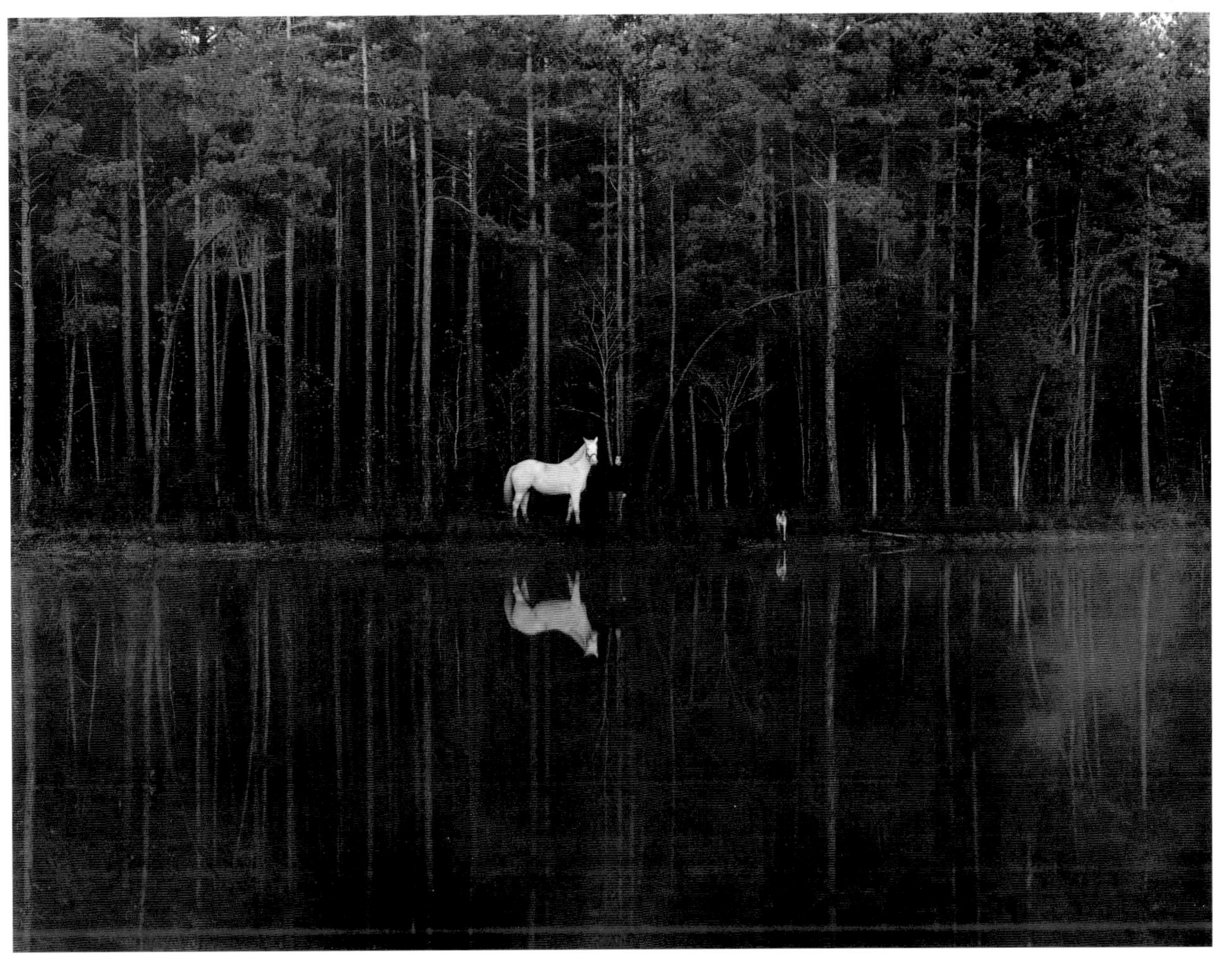

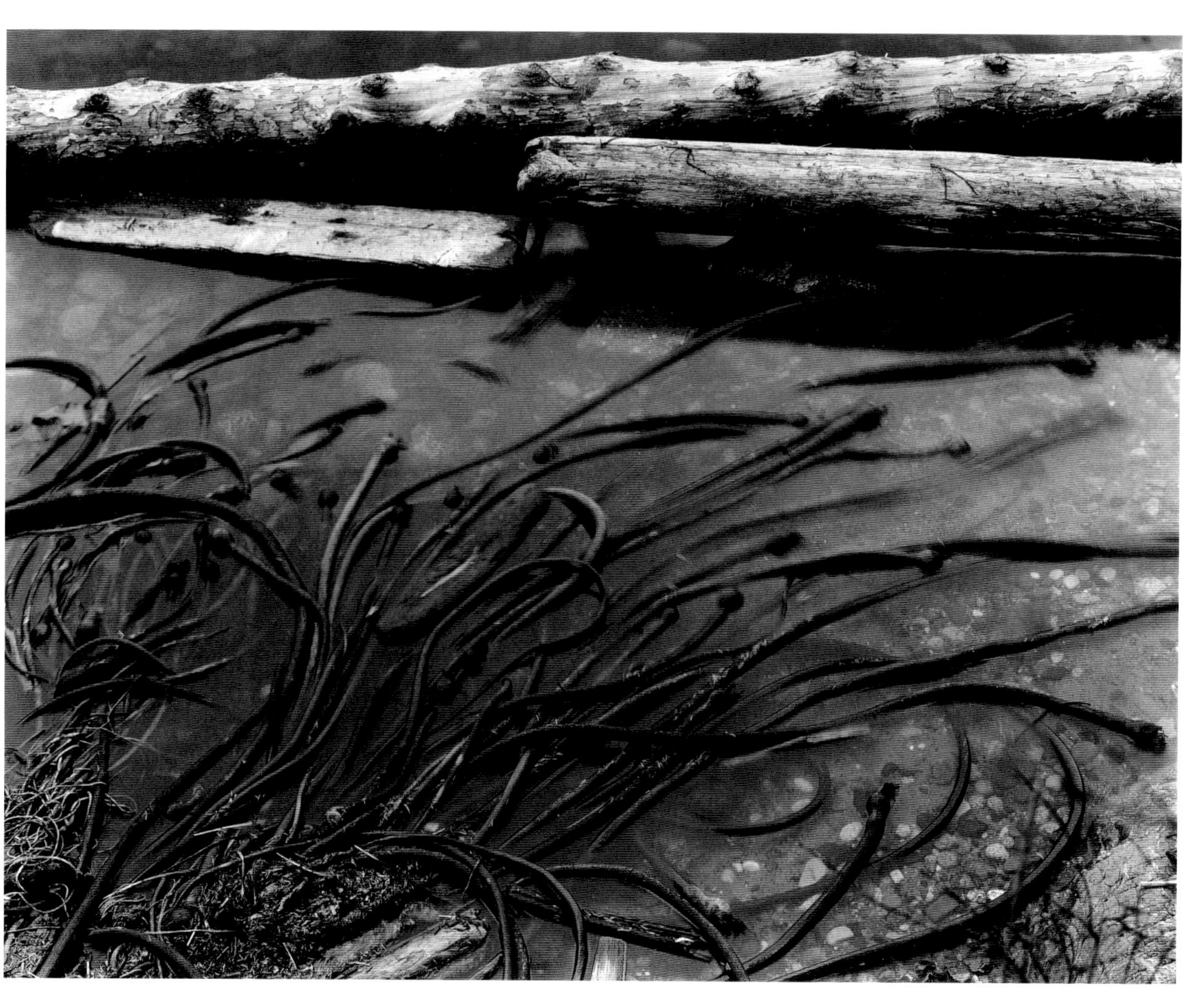

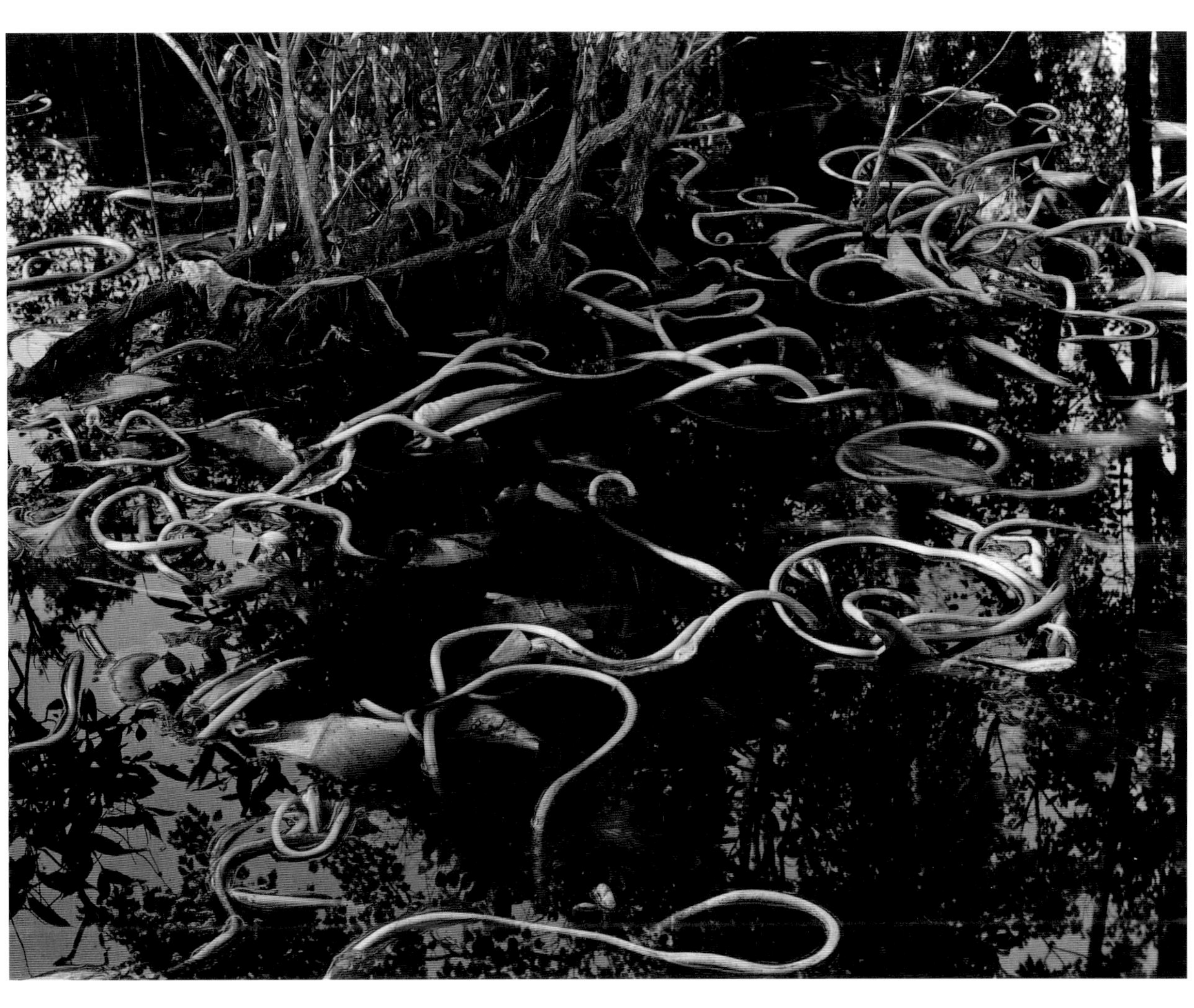

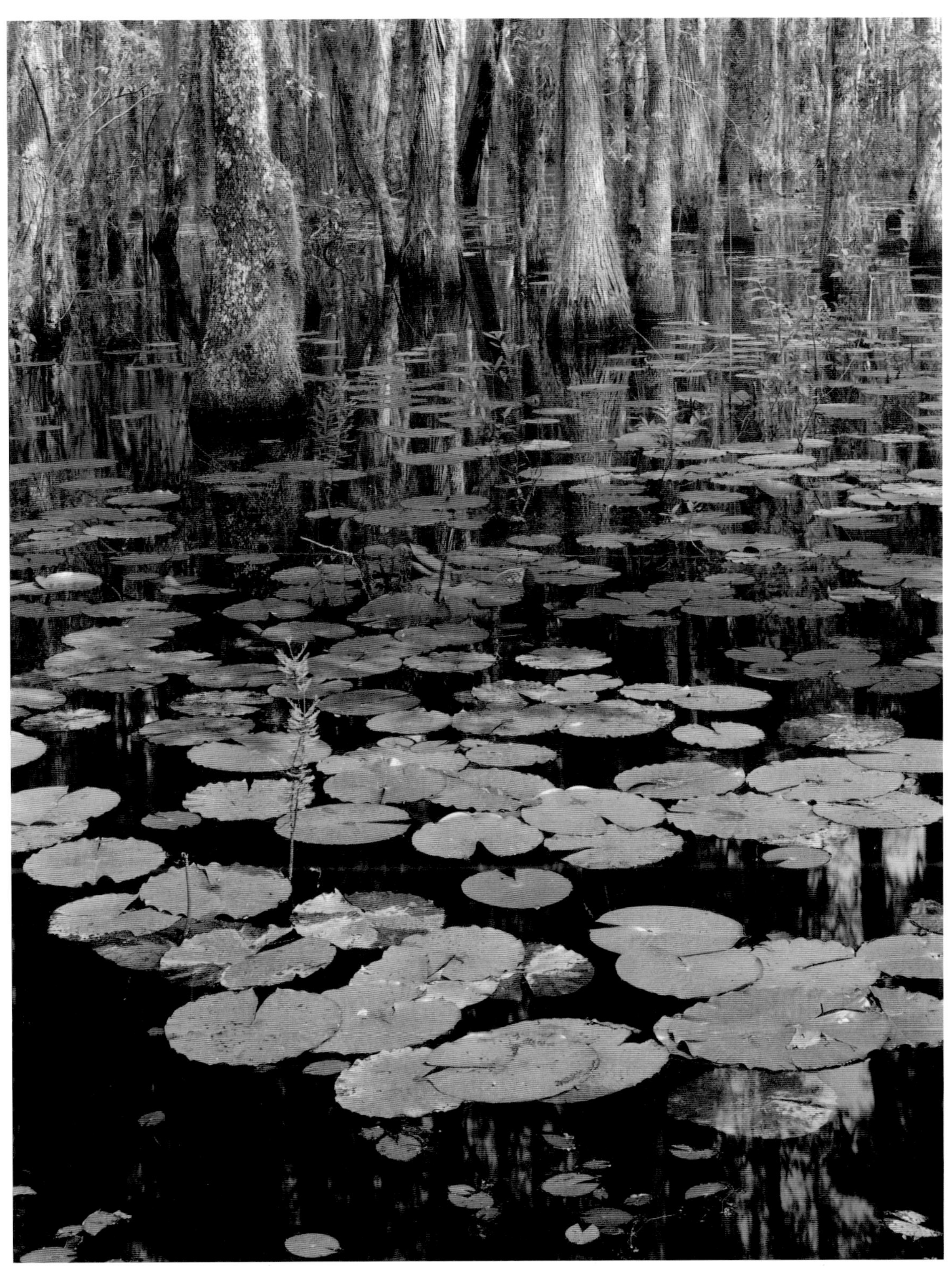

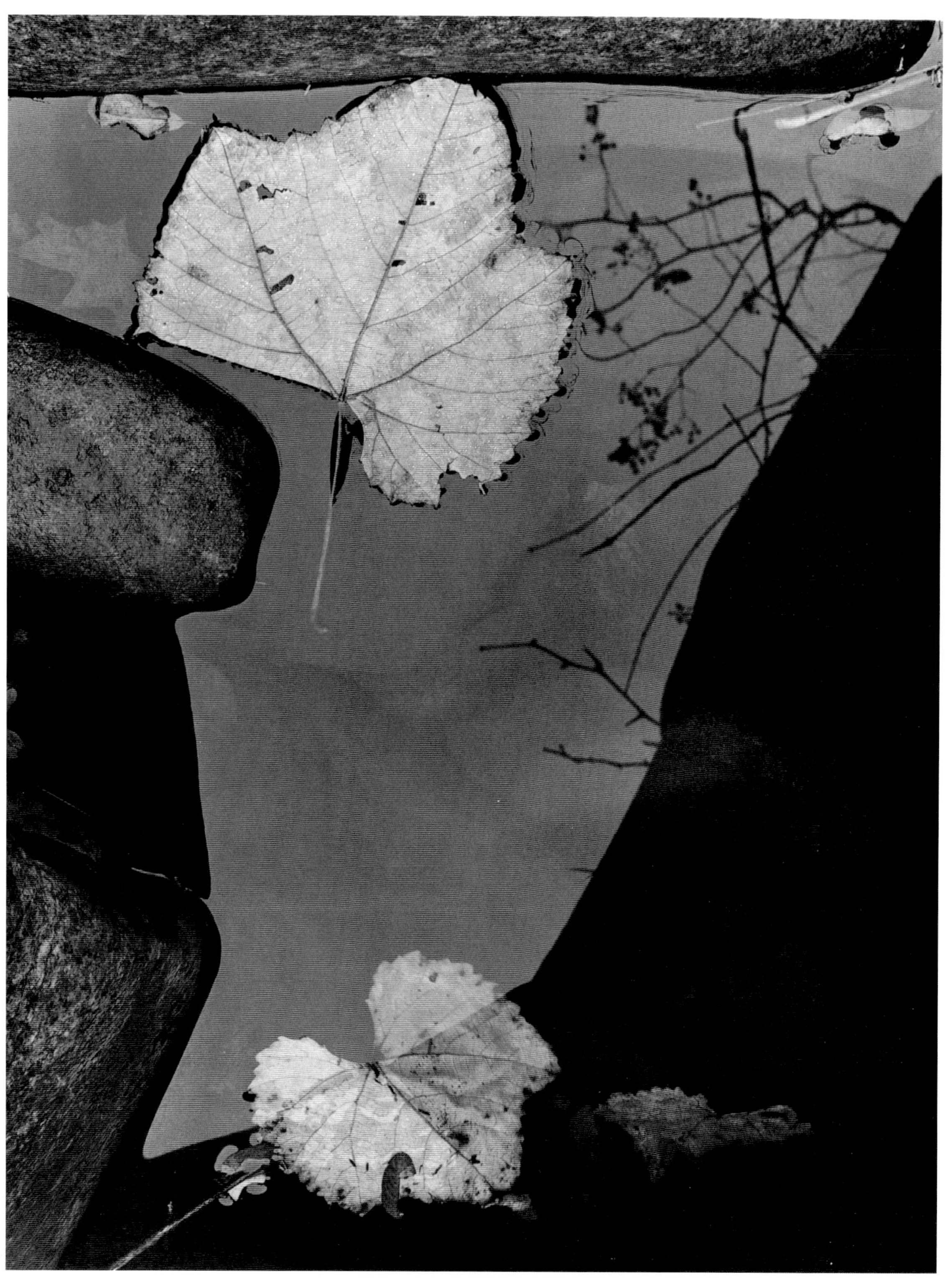

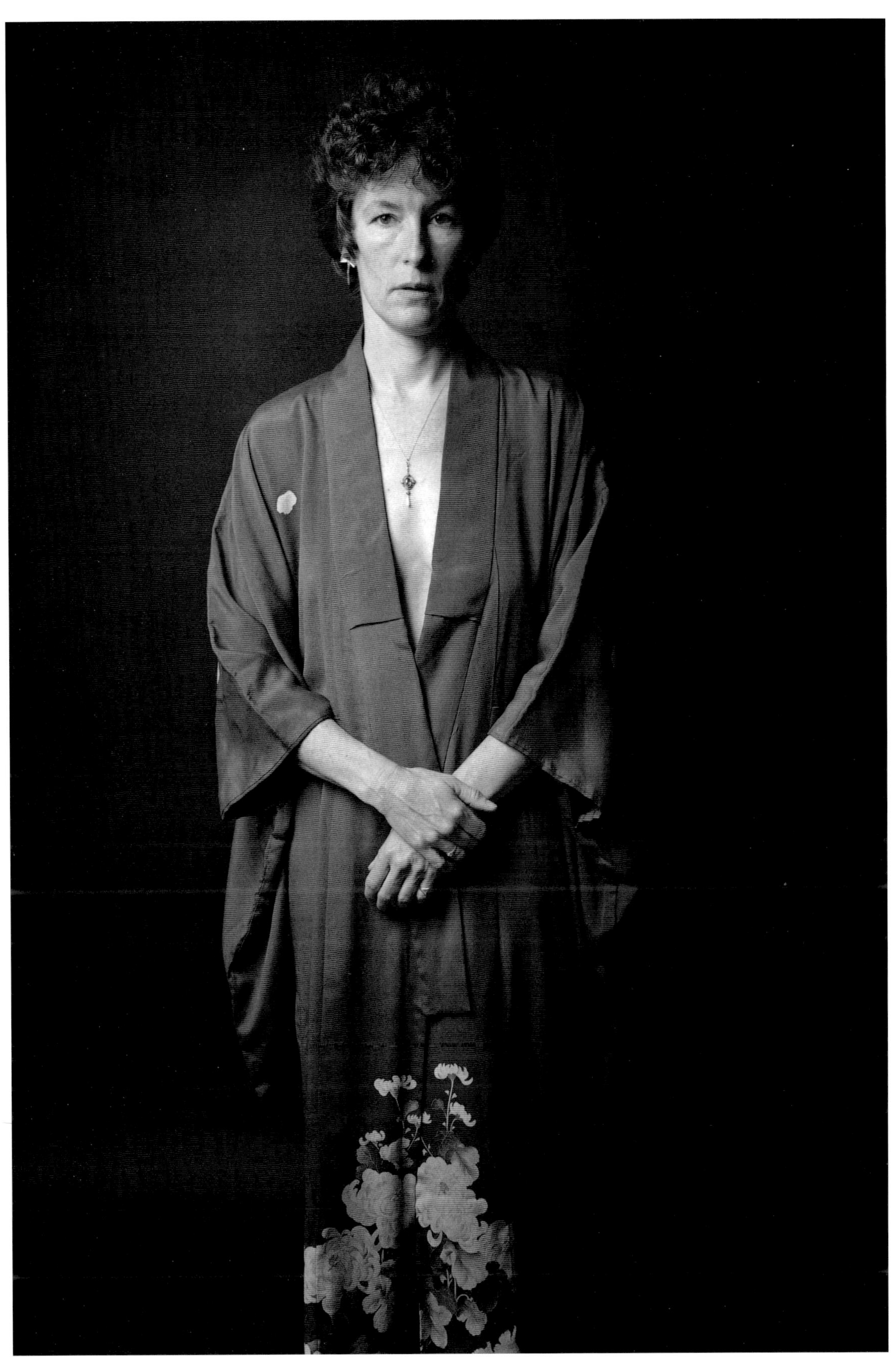

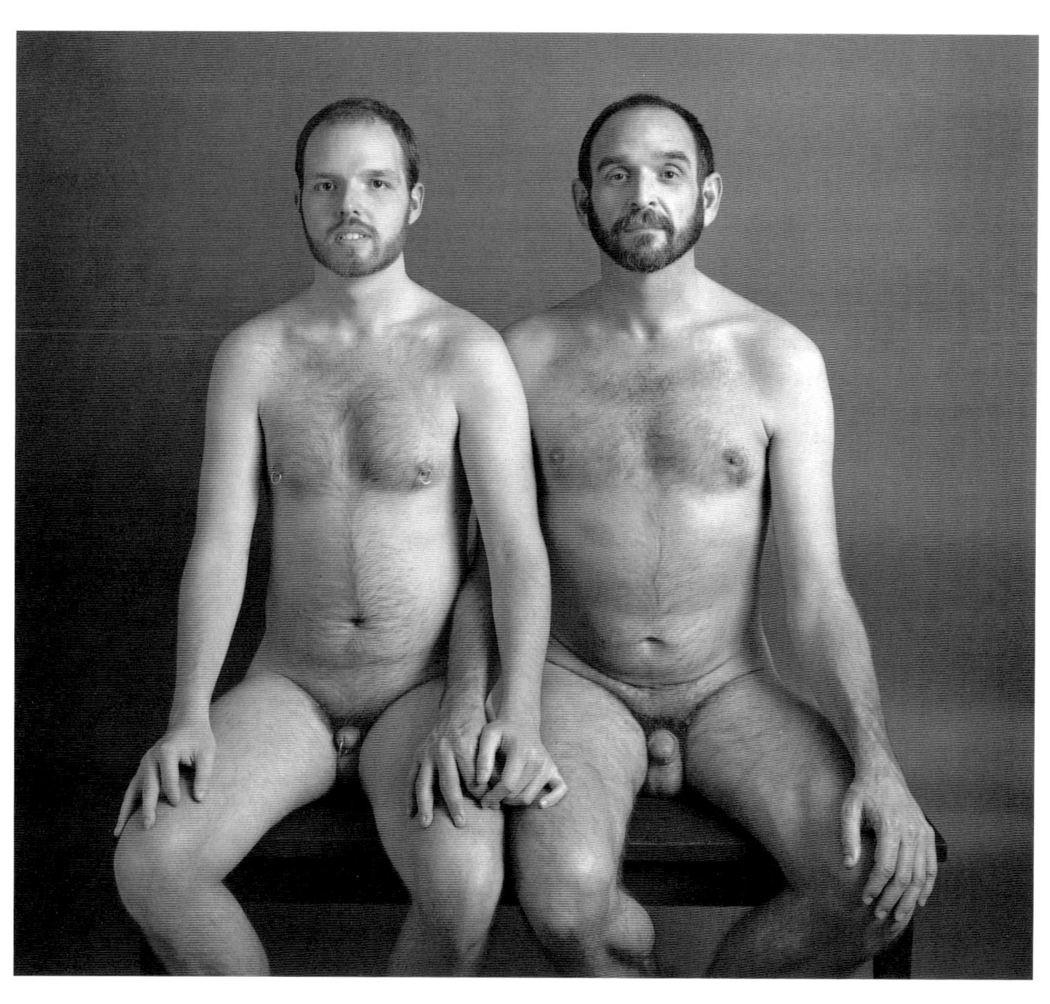

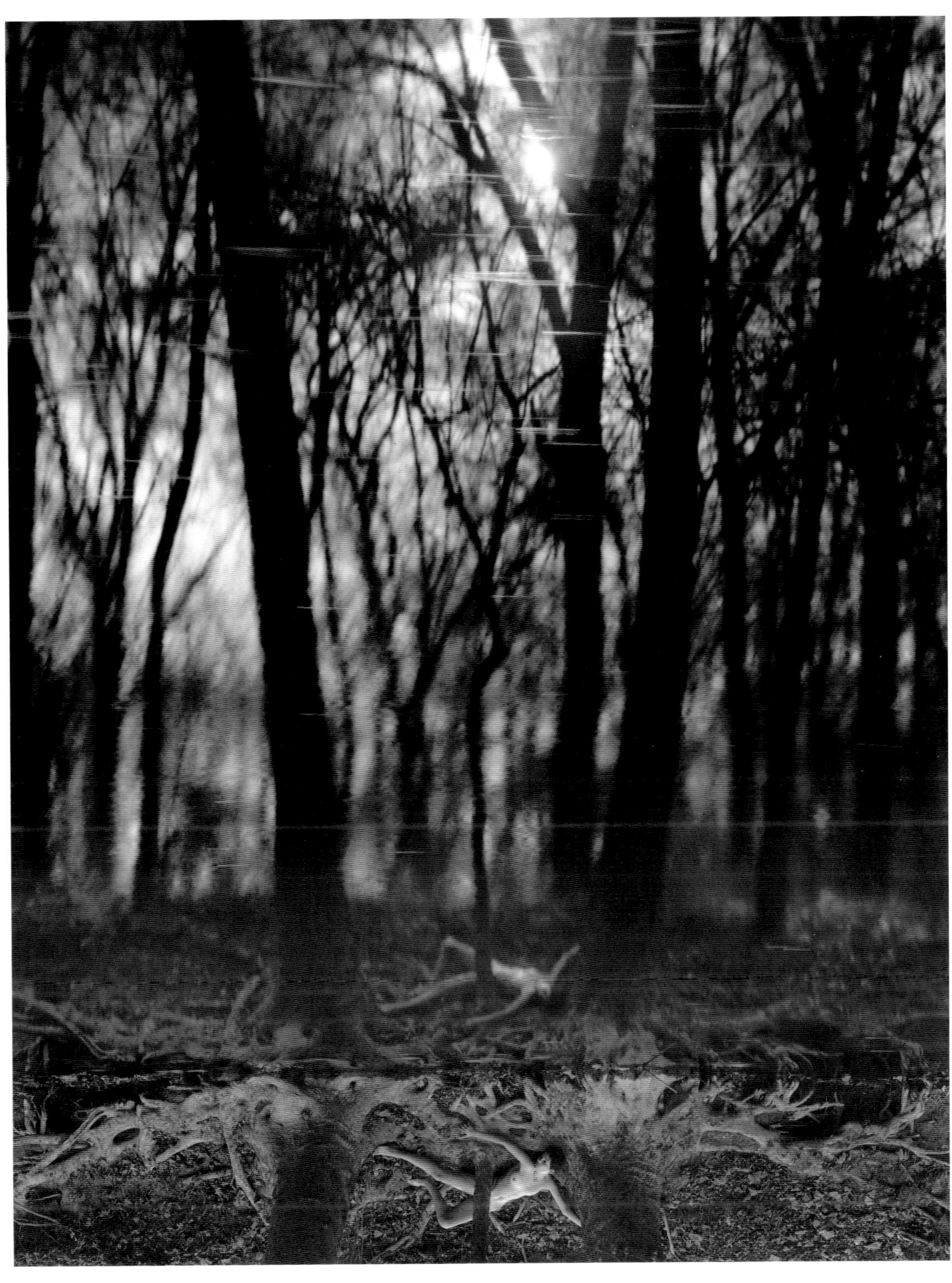

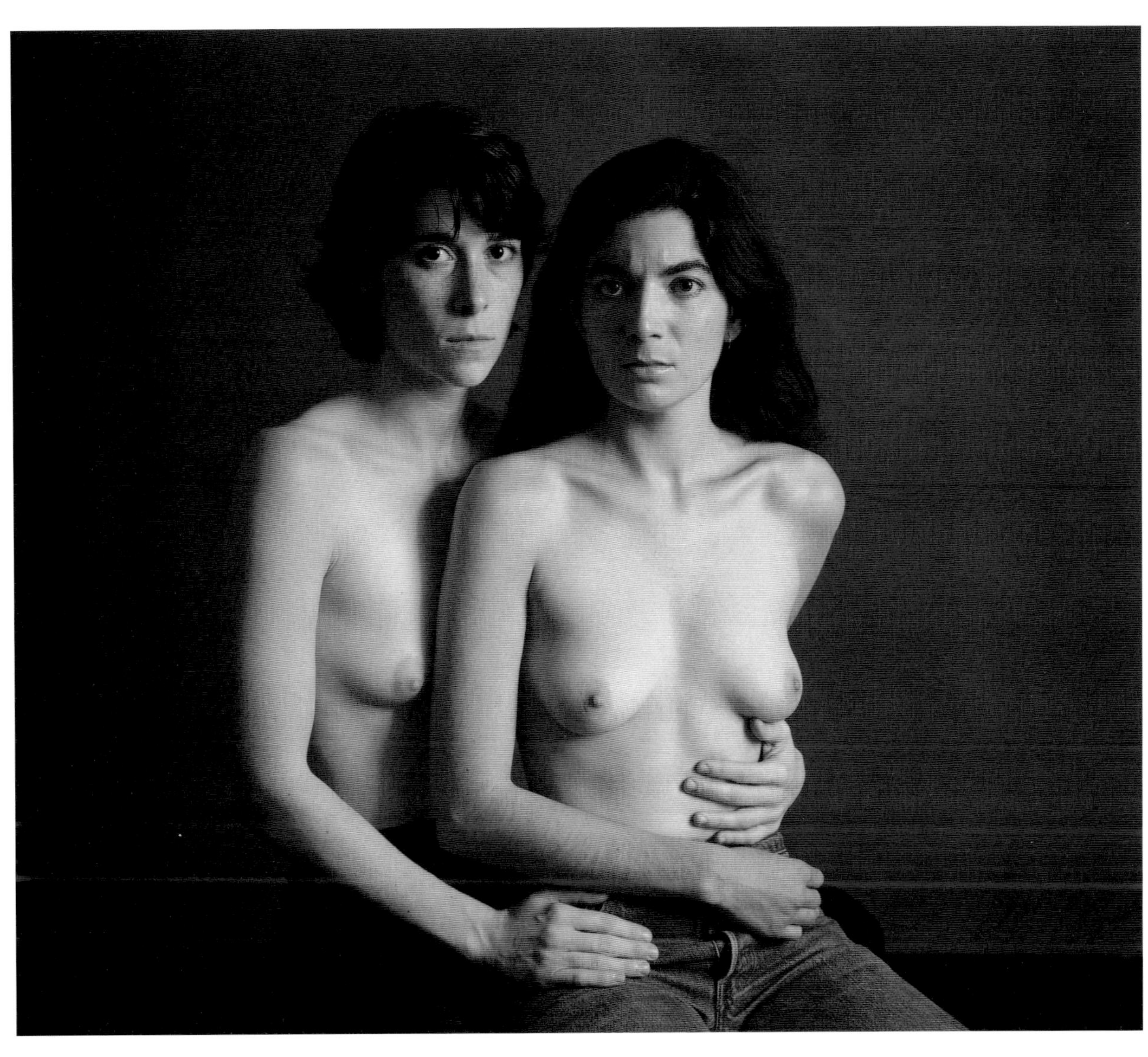

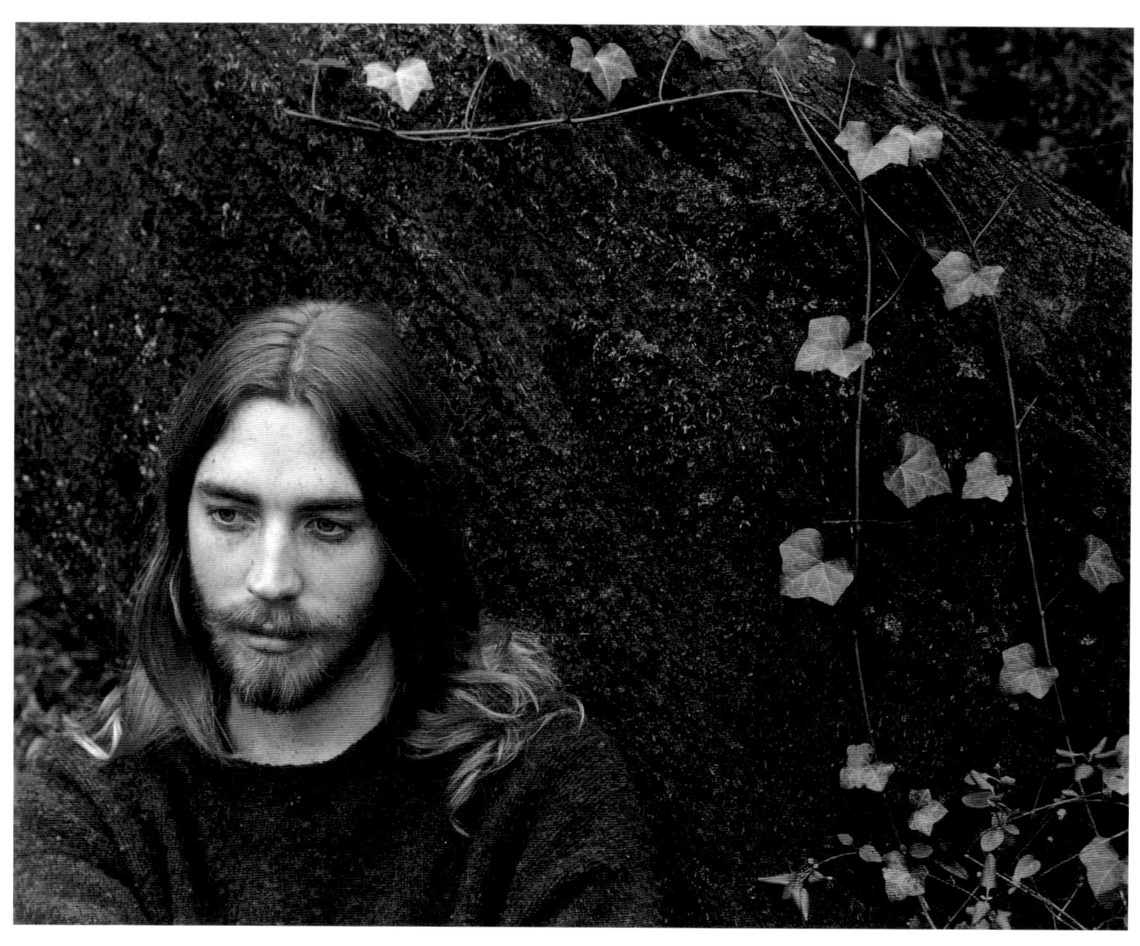

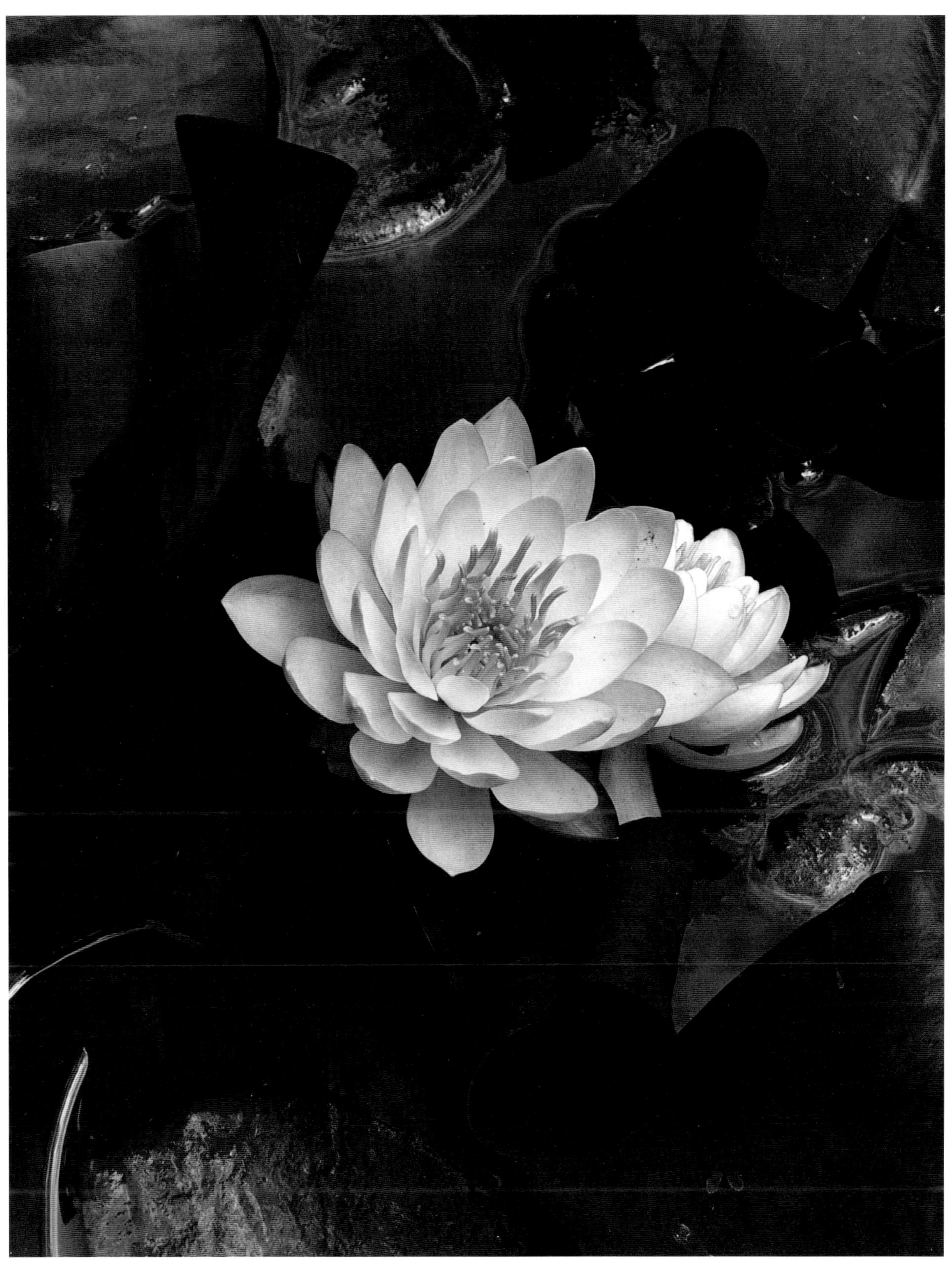

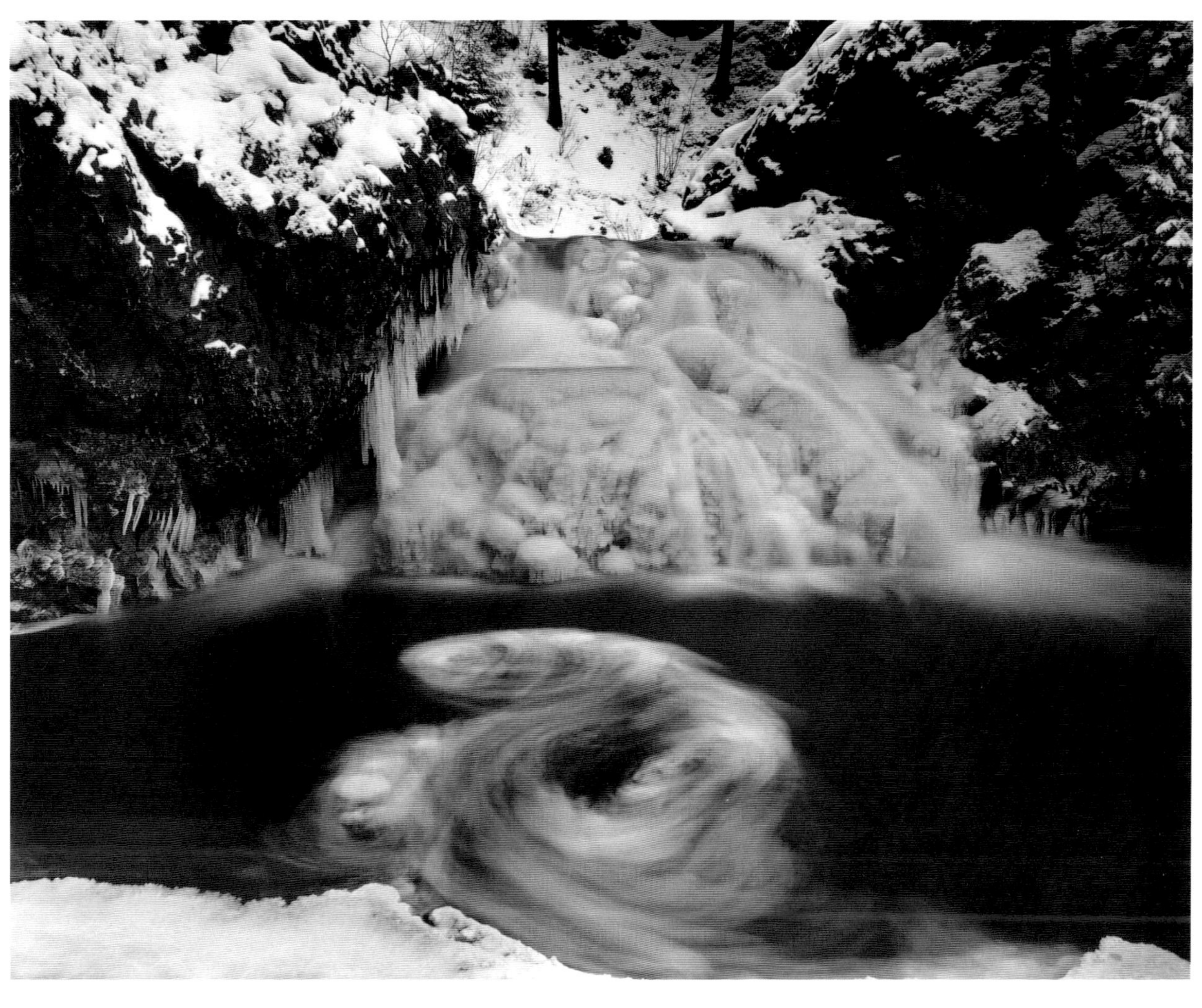

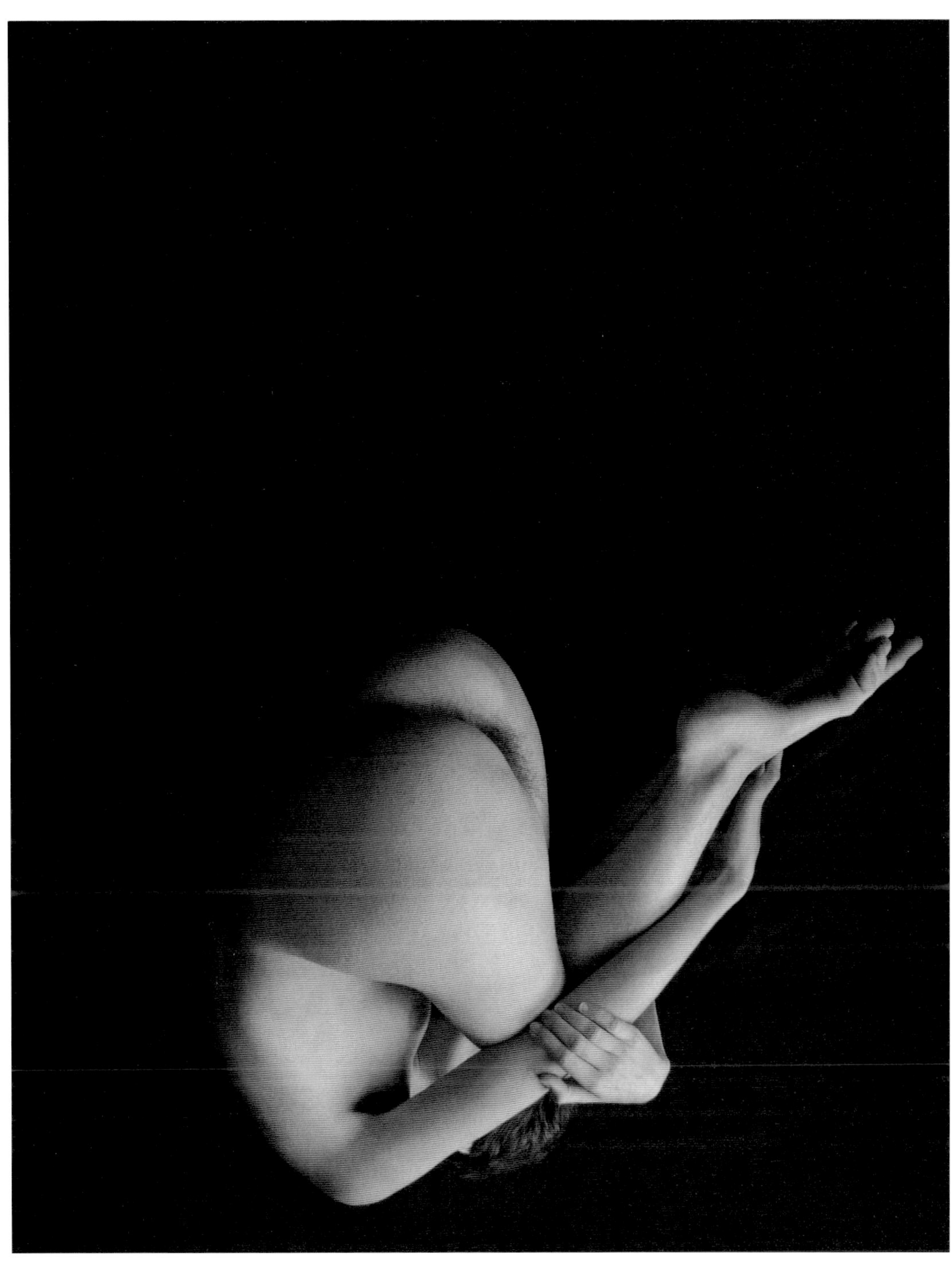

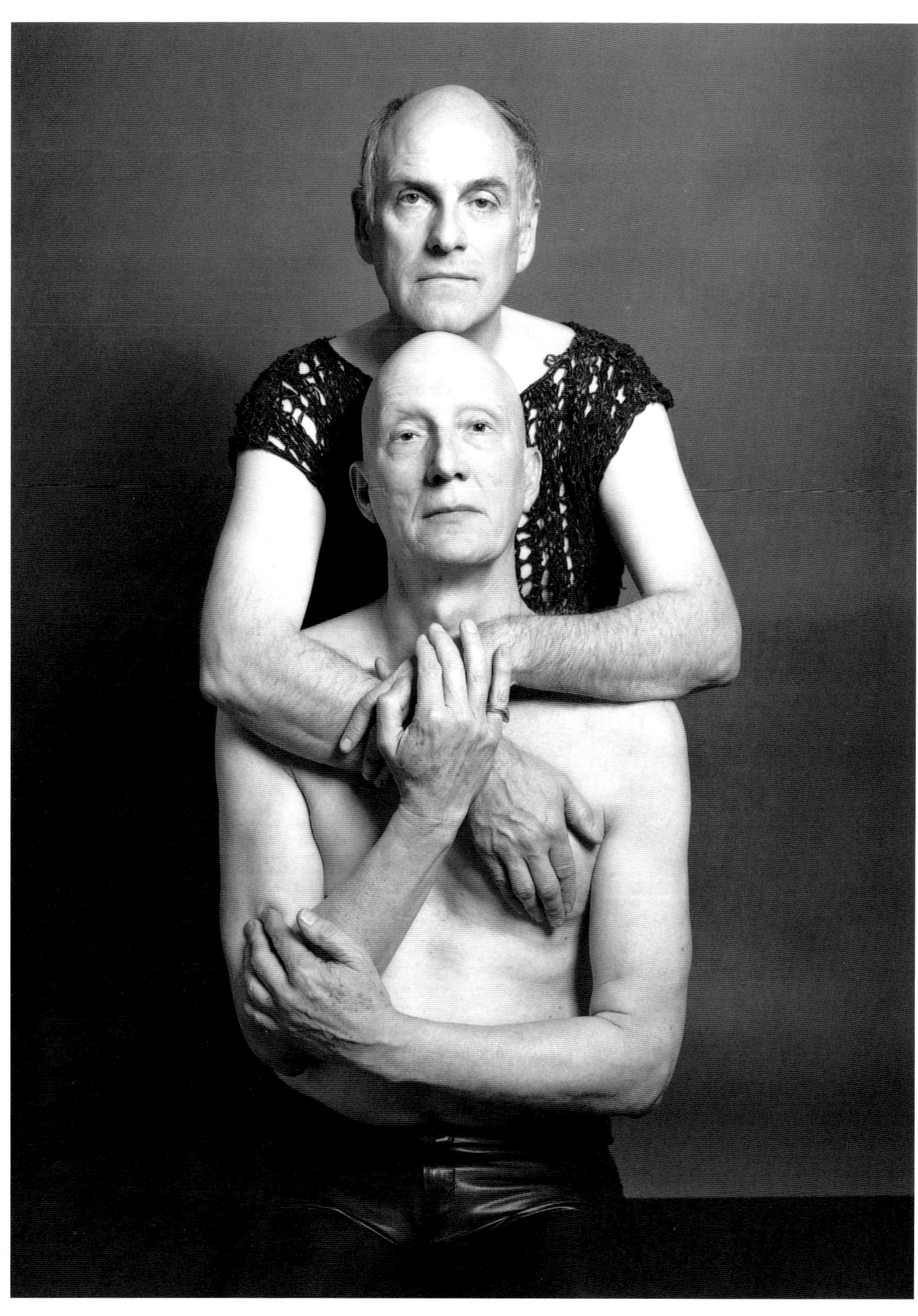

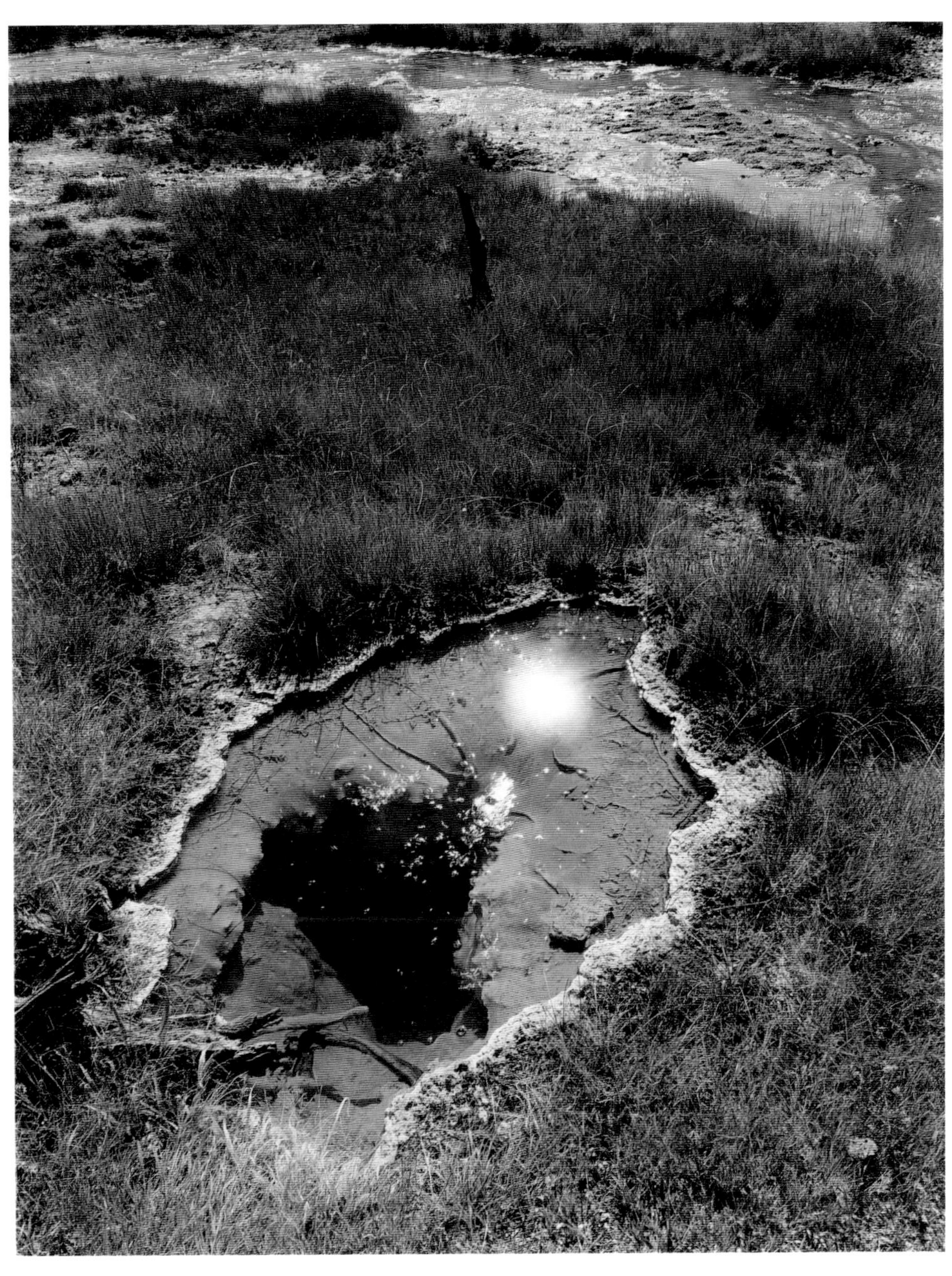

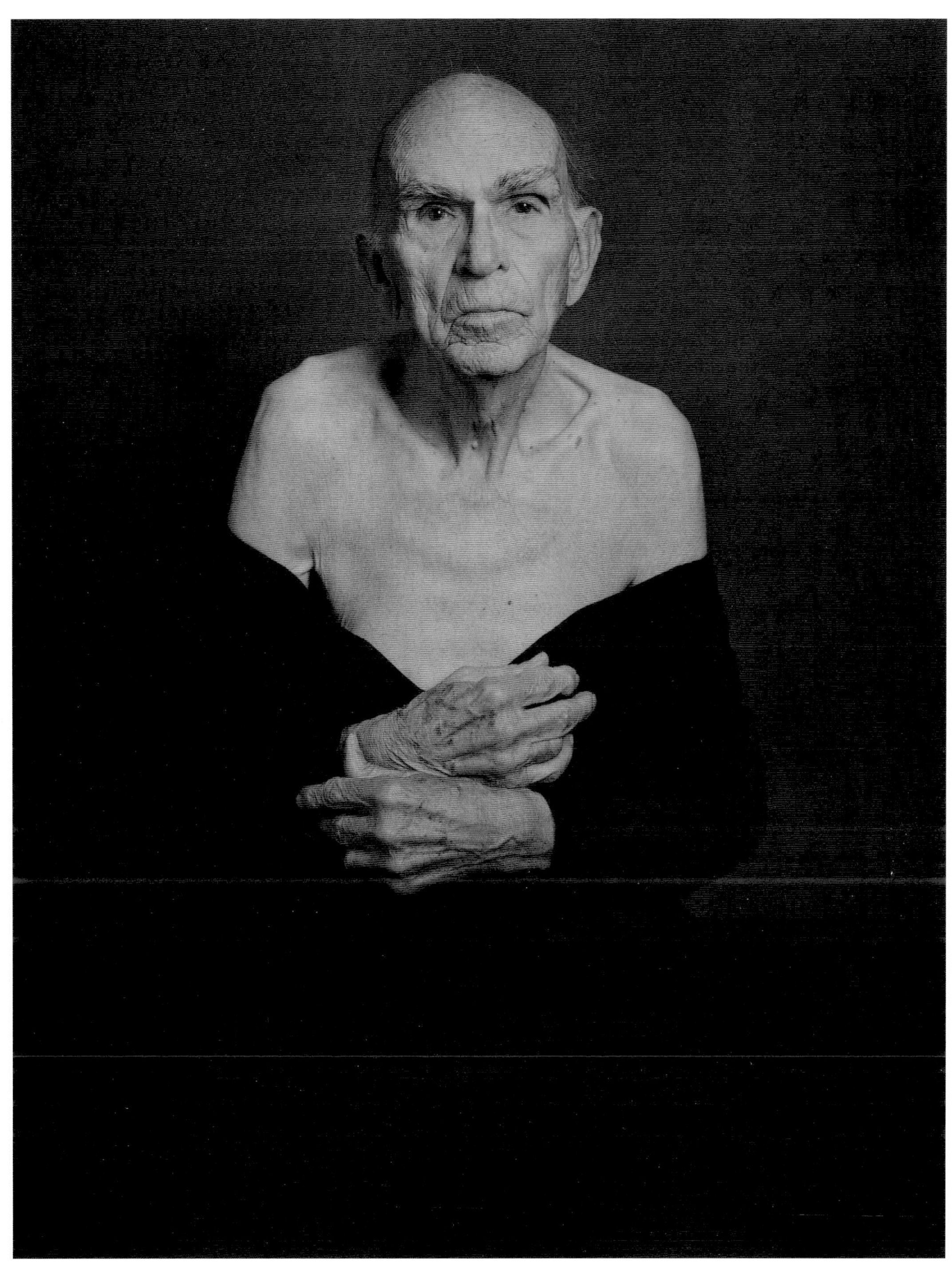

LIST OF PLATES

40 Pomegranate, 1974
41 Lindsay Dearborn Huppé, 1973
43 Great Smokey Mountains, North Carolina [comet rocks], 1974
44 Ripshin Ridge, Tennessee, 1974
45 Edwards County, Texas [dying lamb], 1975
Polaroid PolaPan Type 52 4x5 Land Film
46 Ossabaw Island, Georgia [Middle Earth], 1974
47 Imogen Cunningham [at eighty-eight], 1971
48 Roylee Vaughn Duvall and Barbara Hileman Duvall, June 23, 1990
49 Jeanette and Mary, 1987
51 Jeanette Sarbo, 1972
52 Newfoundland, Canada [sunspot], 1974
53 Journey to Inaccessible Places, Valley of Fire, New Mexico, 1976
54 Dream Waterfall, Ripshin Ridge, Tennessee, 1973
55 Magnolia, 1973
57 Diana's Bath, New Hampshire, 1975
58 Desert Camouflage, Edwards County, Texas, 1976
59 Cottonwood, White Sands, New Mexico, 1976
60 Antediluvian Dream, False Bay, San Juan Islands, Washington, 1975
61 Phoenix Rocks, Gloucester, Massachusetts, 1974
63 An LaBarre, Bonnie and Jody, 1973
64 Kelp, False Bay, San Juan Islands, Washington, 1975
65 Okefenokee Swamp, Georgia, 1974
67 Waterlilies, North Florida, 1974
68 Leaf Synchronicity, 1974
69 Elizabeth Ann, 1987
70 A. G. Wood and Nat Blevins, December 17, 1989
71 Image from a Past Life, 1974
73 Bristol, Vermont, 1971
74 Self-Portrait, Ashdown House, 1971
Polaroid PolaPan Type 52 4x5 Land Film
75 Carol and Teresa, 1989
76 Mickey Bailey, Christmas Eve, 1972
77 Waterlily Celebration, 1974
79 Eskimo Spirit, Mammal Breath, Truro, Nova Scotia, January 1975
81 Chambered Nautilus, 1974
82 Merle and Tom, 1990
83 Pocket Basin, Wyoming [sinkhole], 1975
85 Father, 1993

CAROLINE VAUGHAN

Born in 1949, Caroline Hickman Vaughan grew up and attended public school in Durham, North Carolina. In 1967, her first year of college, Vaughan was admitted to the course of study in Duke University's creative writing program, where she first learned narrative writing from Reynolds Price and the late William Blackburn.

Her studies in photography included the mentorship of John Menapace and work with Murray Riss at North Carolina's Penland School. Vaughan graduated from Duke in 1971 and immediately thereafter traveled to San Francisco to meet Imogen Cunningham. During 1971-72 she participated in a program of intensive study with Minor White at M. I. T. She was the only female among his seven students for that academic year—and received what was to be her most influential instruction in the technical and spiritual nature of her chosen art form.

Her highly personal history of making photographic images includes traversing North America, logging more than 75,000 miles to capture the vastness of nature's space. At the other extreme, she has worked quietly, very close to home, photographing members of her own family as if the universe could be found in their faces and their gestures.

The photographs presented here are a mid-life review of Caroline Vaughan's singular vision, and her effort to interpret the natural world and its human inhabitants.

SELECTED ONE-PERSON EXHIBITIONS

1975 Gallery 218, Memphis, Tennessee.
Saint Mary's University Art Gallery, Halifax, Nova Scotia.

1976 Memorial Union, University of Wisconsin, Madison, Wisconsin.

1977 Center for Photographic Studies, Louisville, Kentucky.
1978 Amon Carter Museum, Fort Worth, Texas.
1986 Duke University Institute of the Arts, Bivins Gallery, Duke University, Durham, North Carolina.
1989 Caldwell Arts Council, Lenoir, North Carolina.
1990 Virginia Intermont College, Bristol, Virginia.

SELECTED GROUP EXHIBITIONS

1971 *Latent Image* (with catalog), Duke University Art Museum, Durham, North Carolina. Vaughan was co-founder of the annual Latent Image exhibition and catalog with John Menapace and Robert Roscow.

North Carolina State Photography Exhibition, Raleigh, North Carolina.

50 Polaroid Prints, Zone V Photographers' Workshop, Watertown, Massachusetts.

1972 *Bi-Annual Print and Drawing Competition*, Winston-Salem Gallery of Contemporary Art, Winston-Salem, North Carolina.

Images of Imogen, Focus Gallery, San Francisco, California.

North Carolina Artists' Exhibition, North Carolina Museum of Art, Raleigh, North Carolina.

The Polaroid Museum Collection, Boston Museum of Fine Arts, Boston, Massachusetts, and the Clarence Kennedy Gallery, Cambridge, Massachusetts.

1974 *Eleven Photographers at the Garden Gallery*, Garden Gallery, Raleigh, North Carolina.

Variety Show 2, organized by Margery Mann, California State University at Humbolt, Arcata, California.

Celebrations, theme show with catalog published by *Aperture*, volume 18, no. 2, organized by Minor White, Hayden Gallery, M.I.T., Cambridge, Massachusetts.

Torrence Street Gallery, three-person show with Nick Dean and Steve Pirelli, Charlotte, North Carolina.

1975 *Women Look At Women*, traveling exhibition organized by Jayne Blankenship Kantor, Lyman Allyn Museum, New London, Connecticut. Other sites included: Photographic Workshop, New Canaan, Connecticut; Carlson Gallery, College of Fine Arts, University of Bridgeport, Bridgeport, Connecticut; (1976) Madison Art Center, Madison, Wisconsin.

42nd Semi-Annual Southeastern Prints-Drawing-Photography Competition, Southeastern Center for Contemporary Art, Winston-Salem, North Carolina.

The Silver Image Gallery Christmas Show, The Silver Image Gallery, Tacoma, Washington.

1976 Neikrug Gallery, New York, New York.

A Temporary Possession: The Human Image in 20th Century Photography, Museum of Art, Washington State University, Pullman, Washington.

1979 *Hot Shots—25 Photographers*, opening for the new Southeastern Center for Contemporary Art, Winston-Salem, North Carolina.

1987 *North Carolina Artists' Exhibition* (with catalog), curated by Roberta Smith, North Carolina Musem of Art, Raleigh, North Carolina.

North Carolina Photography, Gilliam & Peden Art Gallery, Raleigh, North Carolina.

1988 *North Carolina Photographers' Annual*, Meredith College, Gaddy-Hambrick Art Center, Frankie G. Weems Gallery, Raleigh, North Carolina.

Plant Forms from the Amon Carter Collection, Amon Carter Museum, Fort Worth, Texas.

Andrea Modica, Debby Fleming Caffey and Caroline Vaughan, The Light Factory, Charlotte, North Carolina.

The Psychological Landscape, curated by John Rosenthal, Green Hill Center for North Carolina Art, Greensboro, North Carolina.

1989 *New Southern Photography, Between Myth and Reality*, (with catalog) published by *Aperture*, Volume 115, The Burden Gallery, Aperture Foundation, New York, New York.

1990 *Women by Women: Four Contemporary Photographers: Connie Imboden, Jennifer Tucker, Patricia Dalzell and Caroline Vaughan*, Second Street Gallery, Charlottesville, Virginia.

45th North Carolina Artists' Exhibition, 1990 (with catalog), curated by Stephen Westfall, North Carolina Museum of Art, Raleigh, North Carolina.

North Carolina Arts Council Artists Fellowships 1990–1991 (with catalog), curated by Ken Bloom, The Knight Gallery, Spirit Square, Charlotte, North Carolina.

1992 *Southern Environmental* (with catalog), traveling exhibition curated by Gil Leebrick, The Light Factory, Charlotte, North Carolina, 1991. Other sites included: Clemson University, Clemson, South Carolina, 1991; Virginia Intermont College, Bristol, Virginia, 1992; Savannah College of Art and Design, Savannah, Georgia, 1992; Lander College, Greenwood, South Carolina, 1992.

Point of View: Landscapes From The Addison Collection (with catalog), Addison Gallery of American Art, Phillips Academy, Andover, Massachusetts.

1994 *Latent Image Photographers*, curated by William Noland, April 1994, Bivins Gallery, Duke University Institute of the Arts, East Campus, Durham, North Carolina.

1995 *The 1st Triennial Merry Moor Winnett Photography Exhibit*, the Green Hill Center for North Carolina Art, Greensboro, North Carolina.

PUBLIC COLLECTIONS

Addison Gallery of American Art, Andover, Massachusetts
Amon Carter Museum, Fort Worth, Texas
Burroughs-Wellcome Company, Research Triangle Park, Durham, North Carolina
Duke University Special Collections, Perkins Library, Durham, North Carolina
Museum of Fine Arts, Houston, Texas
NationsBank, Charlotte, North Carolina
North Carolina Museum of Art, Raleigh, North Carolina
North Carolina State University, Raleigh, North Carolina
Ossabaw Island Genesis Collection, Ossabaw Island, Georgia
Polaroid Museum Collection, Cambridge, Massachusetts
Qualex, Inc., Durham, North Carolina

R.J. Reynolds Industries, Inc., Winston-Salem, North Carolina
Saint Mary's University, Halifax, Nova Scotia, Canada
University of Wisconsin Student Union, Madison, Wisconsin

SELECTED PUBLICATIONS

1971 *Latent Image*, volumes 1, 1971; 2, 1975; 3, 1976; 11, 1991; 12, 1992; 13, 1993; Duke University Publications Board, Duke University, Durham, North Carolina.

1973 *Aperture*, volume 17, no. 2 (back cover), advertisement for Polaroid.

1974 *Aperture*, volume 18, no. 2, 1974, theme exhibition "Celebrations," 3 photographs.

1975 *Camera*, no. 8 (cover), August 1975, Lucerne, Switzerland, p. 31.

Camera, no. 9, September 1975, Lucerne, Switzerland, p. 20.

Poetry Lives, Green Level, Blue Level (poetry for children), McDougal, Littell and Company, 1975, Evanston, Illinois.

Quest: A Feminist Quarterly, volume 2, no. 1 (cover), 1975, Baltimore, Maryland.

1979 *SX-70 Art*, edited by Ralph Gibson, Lustrum Press, 1979, p. 85.

1980 *Zoom, The International Image Magazine*, from "The Polaroid Story," volume 11, October 1980, Paris, France, pp. 110-114.

Elmatha's Apology (cover, portrait of author Rebecca Ranson), 1985, Carolina Wren Press, Chapel Hill, North Carolina.

1984 *Polaroid Foundation Annual Report 1984/85* (one photograph), Cambridge, Massachusetts.

1986 *Kate Vaiden*, by Reynolds Price (cover, inside portrait of author), 1986, Atheneum, New York.

1987 *The Laws of Ice*, by Reynolds Price (back cover portrait of author), 1987, Atheneum, New York.

1988 *The Night of the Weeping Women*, by Lawrence Naumoff (portrait of the author), 1988, Atlantic Monthly Press.

Good Hearts, by Reynolds Price (portrait of author), 1988, Atheneum, New York.

Real Copies, by Reynolds Price (portrait of the author), 1988, NC Wesleyan College Press, Rocky Mount, North Carolina.

1989 *Clear Pictures*, by Reynolds Price (portrait of the author), 1989, Atheneum, New York.

Doing What Comes Naturally, by Stanley Fish (portrait of the author), 1989, Duke University Press, Durham, North Carolina.

1989 *The Big Click, Photographs of One Day In North Carolina*, April 21, 1989, Lightworks, Raleigh, North Carolina.

1990 *Rootie Kazootie*, by Lawrence Naumoff (portrait of the author), 1990, Farrar, Straus & Giroux, New York.

Aperture, volume 115, "New Southern Photography: Between Myth and Reality," introduction by Reynolds Price, "Neighbors and Kin," (2 photographs), June 1990, New York, p.32 and pp.38-39.

North Carolina Artist's Exhibition Catalogue, North Carolina Museum of Art, July 1987, 1990, Raleigh, North Carolina.

1991 *Parnassus: Poetry in Review*, volume 16, no. 2 (one portrait), June 1991, New York.

1992 *Salt Works*, poems by Mike Chitwood (portrait of the author), 1992, Ohio Review Books, Athens, Ohio.

Taller Women, by Lawrence Naumoff (portrait of the author), 1992, Harcourt Brace Jovanovich, New York.

Point of View: Landscapes From The Addison Collection, Addison Gallery of American Art, Phillips Academy, 1992, Andover, Massachusetts, from the section titled "The Focused View," p. 112.

1993 *The Catalogue of the Amon Carter Museum Photography Collection*, a survey documenting work by 350 artists, edited by Carol E. Roark, Paula Ann Stewart, and Mary Kennedy McCabe, 1993, Amon Carter Museum, Fort Worth, Texas; 16 illus., with biography.

1994 *A Whole New Life*, by Reynolds Price (back cover portrait of the author), 1994, Macmillian, New York.

Parnassus: Poetry in Review, volume 18, no. 2 and 19, no. 1 (one photograph each), from the relationship series, New York.

Duke Magazine, "Telling Stories in the Age of Aids," March-April 1994, Durham, North Carolina.

REVIEWS AND ARTICLES ABOUT CAROLINE VAUGHAN

1979 *The Raleigh News and Observer*, Leisure Living section, "An Artistic View of Photography," by Cole C. Campbell, 29 July 1979, pp. 1, 14.

The Durham Sun, "Vaughan Photos Food for Thought," 16 August 1979, p. 3-D.

The Arts Journal, "Portfolio," by Georgann Eubanks (cover, 6 photographs), volume 5, no. 2, November 1979, pp. 1-4.

1980 *The Arts Journal*, "Self-Portraits," January 1980.

1986 *The Durham Morning Herald*, "Home Ground," by Betty Hodges, 12 October 1986.

Spectator Magazine, "The Old Place," review by John Rosenthal, 23 October 1986.

1987 *Spectator Magazine*, Connoiseur section, "Photography As a Way of Life: The Life and Vision of Caroline Vaughan," by Kim Weiss, September, 1987, pp. 23-26; 4 illus.

A Common Room, Essays 1954-1987, "A World At Least To Love," by Reynolds Price, Atheneum, New York, 1987, pp. 385-388.

1988 *Spectator Magazine*, "Writer to Writer," by Max Steele (photograph and review of photograph), 11 August 1988.

1989 *Aperture*, "Neighbors and Kin," by Reynolds Price, volume 115, 1989, New York.

The Independent Weekly, "Angling for the Elusive," interview by Georgann Eubanks, July 1989.

1990 *Art Papers*, "Caroline Vaughan, Caldwell Arts Council," by Frank Thomson, exhibition review, March/April 1990.

1991 *Art Vu*, Review of the 1990 NCAE NCMA in Raleigh, North Carolina, by Michael Brady, volume 4, no. 2, March 1991.

North Carolina Arts Council Artists Fellowships 1990–1991 (catalog), interview by Ken Bloom, April, 1991.

ACKNOWLEDGMENTS

When I think of all the people who have helped shape my imaginative and creative processes I am struck by the fact that many of them are already deceased: W. K. Stars encouraged me to try photography in high school; Alexander Koplowitz gave me my first darkroom lesson; William Blackburn challenged me to think in terms of story and narrative; both Imogen Cunningham and Minor White served as mentors to me in diametrically opposing ways. Minor White encouraged me to "see" with all of my senses and to make photography a way of life. Imogen Cunningham encouraged me not to study at all, to just "make photographs." These teachers made a lasting impression on my outlook and work. I would also like to pay tribute to two people who allowed me to make portraits when their time was running out: Nat Blevins and Erica VanCourt.

A most special thanks to my parents, Mary and William Vaughan—my most patient and lifelong models.

There is a longer list of people who have encouraged me through the years to work on the images and stories in my heart. John Menapace spent one summer of his life patiently teaching me the technical aspects of photography and sharing with me his keen appreciation of this art form. Other support for my early work came from Chula Reynolds, Whitney Hyder More, Margaret Gibson Nicoll, Stephen Dunn, Georgann Eubanks, Erica Rapport Gringle, Jean Hamilton, and Jane Dolkart. I also wish to thank Sally Mann, Olivia Parker, and Margaret Sartor for their insights and encouragement. For her help I also thank Marjorie Morey, formerly of the Amon Carter Museum.

A special thank you to Anita Mills who helped me with every aspect of this book project. Reynolds Price, Eileen Gordy, Elizabeth Matheson, Jonathan Williams, and Tom Meyer all contributed their expertise. I thank George Smith for his support throughout.

Although the contributions of the Duke Press staff are too numerous to describe here, I would like to thank three people who worked very closely with me for more than two years to produce this book: Reynolds Smith, Sharon Parks, and Mary Mendell. I appreciate the supportive and thoughtful words I received from three reviewers whose insights helped shape this book: Anne Tucker, Curator of Photography at the Museum of Fine Arts in Houston, Texas; Alex Harris, Professor of Practice in Public Policy at the Center for Documentary Studies at Duke University; and Marianne Fulton, Chief Curator, George Eastman House, Rochester, New York. I am especially grateful to Marianne Fulton who assisted with editing the photographs into their final sequence.

I continue to be thankful to the Durham Arts Council, the North Carolina State Arts Board, the Duke University Center for Documentary Studies, and the Polaroid Corporation for their support.

This book was partially funded by Steve and Ruth Wainwright who have encouraged me for more than twenty years. I am grateful to the Alice Kleberg Reynolds Meyer Foundation of San Antonio, Texas, and the Mary Duke Biddle Foundation of Durham, North Carolina, for their grants to support the production costs of this book.

Library of Congress Cataloging-in-Publication Data

Vaughan, Caroline

Borrowed Time / photographs by Caroline Vaughan:

foreword by Reynolds Price

ISBN 0-8223-1825-3 (cloth : alk. paper. —ISBN 0-8223-1817-2 (pbk. : alk. paper)

1. Photography, Artistic. 2. Vaughan, Caroline. I. Title.

TR654.V38 1996 779'.092—DC20 96-12842 CIP